Steve
PUB

# A Wild Australia Guide

# BIRDS

AUTHOR: **LYNNE ADCOCK**
PRINCIPAL PHOTOGRAPHER: **STEVE PARISH**

# Contents

**Below:** Wedge-tailed Eagle (*Aquila audax*).

# Introduction

Birds have fascinated humans since time immemorial. Colourful or drab, cheeky or shy, their liveliness and song attract attention. Occupying almost every corner of the globe, they are easy to encounter and in some places represent the only possible experience of nature. Humans love to watch their behaviour, ranging from the amusing to the downright shocking, and regard with great admiration their ability to fly. For all of these reasons, birds have featured in art and mythology since the Stone Age. In more recent times they have been the most intensely studied of all of the Earth's creatures.

So, what is a bird? Although they vary in their ability to fly, all birds have wings. They are active, warm-blooded (maintain a steady, core body temperature) vertebrates (animals with backbones) with highly efficient metabolisms. They are able to extract large amounts of oxygen from the air, and pump it quickly through their bodies via their large four-chambered hearts. Feathers cover their bodies and provide insulation. They commence their lives as embryos encapsulated in water-resistant shells incubated by their parents. Although the world's almost 10,000 bird species are highly diverse in their size, shape, plumage and lifestyles; all share these characteristics, which distinguish them from their closest relatives, the reptiles.

## OVER THE AEONS

Scientists believe that birds evolved from reptile-like animals, possibly insectivorous, tree-dwelling dinosaurs. The earliest-known fossil bird, the *Archaeopteryx*, lived about 150 million years ago. It had feathers, wings and the toothed jaws of a carnivorous reptile. The oldest known beaked bird, discovered in China and named Confuciusornis, was a plant-eater. Lacking the keeled breastbones of modern birds, these ancient birds were probably not strong flyers. Developments enabling more efficient flight are believed to have evolved later. Survivors of the environmental cataclysm 65 millions years ago diversified into the forms alive today.

**Top:** Banded Stilts flying together in formation.
**Right:** Penguins' wings are used for "flying" underwater. **Opposite:** Female Yellow-bellied Sunbird at its nest.

# Classifying Birds

Within the class Aves, birds can be divided into about 29 orders, and then into numerous families, based on their relationships. One of the orders — the passerines or "perching birds"— contains about 60% of the world's almost 10,000 bird species. The other 28 orders, collectively known as non-passerines, each contain 1–380 species. Representatives of 21 orders and 98 families occur in Australia.

The passerines possess four toes, three of them pointing forwards and one backwards. Ending in sharp, moderately curved claws, each can move separately. Their ratchet-like tendons lock the toes, ensuring a secure grip on branches of various sizes, even when asleep. Many passerines are "songbirds", producing complex "songs" of distinct rhythm and structure. In these species, the vocal organ, or syrinx, is more highly developed. Enormously diverse, the generally small passerines range from crows and ravens (65 cm long) to Java's tiny Pygmy Tit (*Psaltria exilis*), only 8 cm long. Most live amongst trees and shrubs, some on the ground and a few almost entirely on the wing.

The non-passerines are a motley group of extremely diverse families, ranging from the Ostrich (*Struthio camelus*, up to 2.8 m high) to the smallest hummingbird (6.3 cm long including its beak). They possess a variety of toe arrangements and/or webbing between their toes. Fewer or shorter toes enable ground birds to run unhindered whereas waders' long toes spread their weight over mud or lily pads. Swimming birds have webbing between some or all of their toes.

Birds that squat on branches have two toes facing forwards and two pointing backwards. Some non-passerines, such as parrots, can reverse their outer toes to use them as feeding aids. Parrots also rotate their feet when climbing. Possessing less developed syrinxes, non-passerines usually do not "sing" in the same sense that passerines do, although they may be extremely vocal.

Both groups are enormously diverse and widely distributed around the Earth.

**Top:** Superb Fairy-wren.  **Right:** Gouldian Finch.

6

## A NOTE ABOUT BIRD NAMES

Birds have been studied over the years, with a variety of names. To avoid confusion, species are given official common names, distinct from the unofficial local common names that differ from localities. Scientific names also change as new research provides new evidence of links between bird species. Here, the accepted checklist is the *Handbook of Australian, New Zealand and Antarctic Birds* (Oxford University Press, Melbourne, 1990) with Christidis & Boles (1994) amendments (www. birdsaustralia.com, 2003).

**Clockwise from top:** The feet of non-perching birds vary due to lifestyle — the jacana's feet are designed for wetland life; The Pacific Gull's feet are perfect for paddling at sea; The cassowary's feet are made to walk through tropical rainforest.

# Feathers & Flight

Adaptations for flight are defining characteristics for most birds. Their strong bodies are streamlined, front limbs have been modified into wings and rear limbs strengthened for launching and landing. Light hollow bones are reinforced with internal struts; some are fused. Most have a large keel on the breastbone — powerful flight muscles attach to this. The attachment of tail feathers to the shortened and fused tailbones (the "parson's nose") provides manoeuvrability. Fused wrist and hand bones support the primary flight feathers; the secondary flight feathers attach to the forearm. The high heartbeat rate and air sacs (connected to the lungs) in many of the bones increase oxygen uptake during flight.

Feathers are complex structures of keratin, the protein comprising mammalian hair and reptilian scales. They have different functions related to insulation, waterproofing and flight. Long and rigid, asymmetrical primary flight feathers provide lift. Long and symmetrical tail flight feathers are used for steering. With barbs that intermesh, flight feathers withstand enormous air pressures. Smaller softer "contour" feathers provide a streamlined covering and waterproofing. Warmth is provided by an underlay of down feathers. Small songbirds may have only 1000 feathers, while larger birds, for instance swans, may have more than 25,000.

## "LIFT-OFF"

Birds' wings are aerodynamically shaped or concave to achieve "lift". When birds contract their wing muscles, the resulting downward stroke of the wings creates forward movement and this in turn creates lift. The larger a bird's wings and the faster its forward speed, produced via the flapping of the wings, the stronger this upward force is. Flapping is therefore used to take off, to fly quickly and to ascend. When gliding, birds save energy but slowly lose speed and height, since they are not creating lift. Soaring is achieved by riding on thermals or updraughts.

Wing shape determines speed and agility and tail shape determines manoeuvrability. Long wings provide efficient flight over long distances.

**Top:** Frigatebirds have forked tails facilitating swift changes in direction.
**Above:** Broad rounded wings provide acceleration and lift.

## A FEATHERED APPEARANCE

Feather pigments create markings, such as banding, spotting, blotching or edging. The overall appearance or plumage of a bird is formed by the combined pattern of all its feather markings. Colour varies between individuals and a few species have different colour forms.

In some species, plumage patterns provide camouflage and protection from predators. In others, certain feathers are distinctively coloured and used as visual signals to indicate a bird's age, gender, breeding condition and social status. These feathers may be visible at appropriate times, often during elaborate displays, and concealed at others. Some species have specialised display plumes for courting purposes. Other species moult and acquire alternate breeding and non-breeding plumage. When alarmed, some species signal danger by twitching or flashing certain feathers. In some species, for example, the Pacific Black Duck (*Anas superciliosa*), some areas of plumage, in this case the speculum, are iridescent or reflective so that they appear different colours in different lights.

Some birds also have areas of unfeathered skin or soft parts, particularly around their heads. These are coloured by pigmentation or blood flow, and may vary with age, gender, mood and breeding readiness.

### THE PARTS OF BIRDS

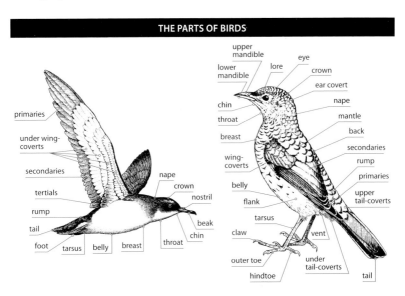

# Senses & Diet

With well-developed brains and finely tuned central nervous systems, birds have powerful senses. Some birds possess more acute eyesight than any other animal. In general, they rely primarily on their exceptional vision to find food, nesting sites and mates, repel intruders and evade predators. With colour vision more highly developed than that of humans, it is little wonder birds communicate by colour signalling. Birds are also finely tuned to sounds, over a similar range of wavelengths as humans, as evidenced by the prevalence of birdsong. Keen hearing enables them to hear the calls of offspring and mates and sense the approach of predators and intruders. A few, including cave-dwelling swiftlets (order: Apodiformes), use echolocation to navigate. Migratory species apparently navigate using a combination of their internal body clocks, memories and the ability to detect variations in the Earth's magnetic field. Birds' senses of smell and taste are less developed.

## FEEDING

In order to fly and maintain their warm-blooded metabolisms, birds need an abundance of energy-rich food each day. They use a range of foraging behaviours to acquire it as quickly and safely as possible. Diets vary widely. Some birds are herbivorous, eating seeds, fruits, nectar, grasses and/or algae. Carnivores feast on invertebrates including molluscs, insects, crustaceans and worms, or smaller vertebrates such as fish, frogs, reptiles, small mammals and birds. Omnivores eat both plants and animals. Scavengers mainly eat carrion. Some partake widely of Nature's smorgasbord while others are more specialised. Most are fairly adaptable. Birds need to drink water regularly.

Birds' beaks and feet reflect their food preferences and foraging behaviours. Leaf litter foragers have large feet and pointy bills. Nectar feeders insert their slender beaks into flowers and lap nectar with brush-tipped tongues. Many parrots manipulate hard-shelled nuts between their feet and exceptionally strong beaks. Birds-of-prey grasp animals in their talons and tear them apart using heavy hooked bills. Pelicans swim using enormous webbed feet and sift schools of fish into their expansive bills.

**Opposite:** Barn Owl chicks feeding on a rodent.
**Above, clockwise from top:** Rainbow Lorikeet feeding on nectar; Rufous Whistler with captured praying mantid; Western Bowerbird feeding on fruit; Australian Ringneck feeding on acacia seeds; Australian Pelican with a beak full of octopus.

Both jaws of birds' bills can move, allowing them to ingest large prey. The digestive system is designed for rapid consumption of food, with extra storage space — the crop. Rapid processing or grinding occurs within the thick muscular gizzard, aided by swallowed grit. Birds' digestive systems also allow for regurgitation of food for their young, or of indigestible parts of their prey.

# Breeding & Ecology

The reproductive cycle begins by establishing a territory and finding a mate. Most birds are monogamous; pair bonds may last a single breeding season or be more permanent. Generally, males take the initiative in courtship — singing, dancing or "displaying" in elaborate rituals, and often chasing females. Courtship may last for several hours, weeks or months. Mating may take place only once or repeatedly.

Nests provide shelter and warmth for eggs and hatchlings. They vary enormously from bare scrapes in the earth to floating rafts to cliff holes or elaborately woven nests. One or both parents build the nest from readily available materials. Some species nest in large colonies, and others are solitary nesters. Clutch sizes vary with females' age, condition and environmental situation. Incubating parents transfer heat to eggs via contact with bare brood patches on their bellies. Incubation lasts 1–12 weeks. Eggs vary in size (0.35–1.5 kg), colour and shape but contain all that is needed for the growth of the embryos: protection, an energy rich food supply (the yolk), gas exchange through the eggshell and room to grow.

Chicks hatch from their shells using a temporary egg tooth at the tip of the upper beak. Some hatch naked and blind and are completely dependent on their parents for warmth until they fledge. Others have a downy covering and are able to walk almost immediately. They require less parental care since more energy was invested in them at the egg stage. Although some are able to forage on their own, most chicks need to be fed so bonding between chicks and parents is essential. Either one or both parents invest all of their energies in raising offspring, teaching them how to forage and recognise danger as they near independence. In some species other adults assist.

Breeding cycles vary with lifespan. Small species with short life spans (5–10 years) usually lay large clutches and provide short-term parental care. Larger birds that live to 50 years usually lay fewer eggs but invest in longer periods of parental care. A few provide no parental care. Survival rates also vary.

**Above:** Black Swan courtship.  **Right:** Red-tailed Tropicbird parental care.  **Opposite:** Wedge-tailed Eagle eating carrion.

## BIRD POPULATIONS

Food availability is of prime concern to birds. Breeding is usually timed to coincide with availability of food supplies, to support the energy demands of parenting. Where regular seasons occur, breeding is usually an annual event; some species have longer cycles. In arid regions with erratic weather, birds tend to breed in response to rain, and their numbers fluctuate accordingly. Subject to changing environmental conditions, bird populations tend to be more stable where conditions are stable or predictable.

Predators also regulate bird populations. As eggs, chicks or adults, birds are preyed upon by a myriad of larger vertebrates including lizards, snakes, carnivorous mammals and larger birds including birds-of-prey. Birds are most susceptible to predation during breeding, especially while nest building and feeding young. Nest hygiene is important; parents remove nestlings' droppings, taking care not to reveal the nest to predators.

Competition and aversion to overcrowding limit reproductive rates. Human-induced environmental changes also impact strongly on bird populations.

## ECOLOGICAL ROLES OF BIRDS

As birds feed on a variety of foods, they in turn play a number of roles within the ecosystems they inhabit. Nectar feeders carry pollen from flower to flower as they forage. Many fruit-eating birds are significant seed dispersers. Insects are an important part of many birds' diets, particularly during breeding, as they are a valuable source of protein and easier for chicks to digest than seeds. Similarly birds that feed on frogs, reptiles, mammals and other birds play a role in regulating their populations too. Carrion eaters carry out the unenviable task of cleaning up the carcasses of dead animals.

# Social Behaviour

Possessing large well-developed brains, birds are blessed with a natural intelligence. In order to feed, reproduce and avoid predators, they engage in social interactions with widely varying degrees of sociability. Some species are solitary or live in pairs, congregating with others for feeding, breeding, roosting or migration purposes. Others are more gregarious, spending their lives in large groups and breeding in enormous colonies or rookeries. Some live in smaller family groups that cooperate to feed chicks during breeding season; others co-opt juveniles from previous clutches to help. Predators or other species that are less vulnerable rarely flock and birds that hunt solitary prey are usually solitary themselves.

Flocking is believed to offer many advantages, including: increased security via advanced warning of predators and safety in numbers; increased opportunity to find mates; and opportunities for cooperative feeding and communal or cooperative breeding. When migrating, flocks save energy by flying in formation and alternating the lead; when moulting they huddle and share body warmth. Disadvantages of the gregarious lifestyle include competition during lean times and the threat of epidemics.

## GROOMING & MOULTING

Birds regularly preen — clean, oil and reshape feathers — using their beaks, to ensure they function efficiently. Feathers are replaced at least once every year, during moulting. Some species moult twice each year, alternating between distinctive breeding plumage and non-descript, non-breeding plumage.

**Top:** Little Corellas preening.  **Above:** Crested Tern breeding colony.
**Opposite:** The Australian Magpie has an extensive melodious repertoire.

## COMMUNICATION

Birds need to communicate to survive. As sound travels well over a distance, it is an effective mode of communication in most habitats. After hearing their parents' calls from inside their eggs, most chicks hatch with a natural ability to recognise and produce the calls of their own species and quickly learn to respond to their parents' calls. Chicks call and posture for food, then learn to forage and avoid danger via warning calls from their parents. Adult birds use sound to proclaim their identity, advertise territory, attract mates or repel competitors or intruders. Most species have unique alarm calls and many are consummate mimics.

Bird sounds vary dramatically. Some non-passerines produce sound mechanically, for example, by clapping their bills (Black-necked Stork, *Ephippiorhynchus asiaticus*) or wings together (Paradise Riflebird, *Ptiloris paradiseus*) or by beating sticks against hollows (Palm Cockatoo, *Probosciger aterrimus*). Most birds use their voices. Sounds range from single note calls to complex songs, produced by vibrating membranes in the syrinx and sometimes amplified in inflatable throat sacs. Songbirds' highly developed syrinx allows them to sing songs of distinct rhythm and structure. Each species has defining songs. Some young birds learn these by imitation; in other species the ability seems to be innate. Individual birds add their own flourishes to the species' song so that it develops over time. In some species, birds living in different localities sing variations of the species' song, referred to as family songs or dialects, which may change over time. In many species, only the males sing; in others, pairs perform duets. Some songbirds sing at night and some seem to sing in "joie-de-vivre!"

Much bird communication is also visual, involving species recognition by plumage, colour signals and displays to attract mates, and alarm behaviour to warn others of approaching predators.

# Migration

Nearly half of the world's bird species divide their time between two or more main locations. Birds cannot necessarily meet their needs — suitable temperatures, abundant food supply and nesting materials — by staying in one place year round.

Sedentary or resident birds spend their entire lives in one area, moving only short distances in response to environmental changes, or dispersing after breeding. More mobile species may move irregularly in response to rainfall and food supply; these are known as nomadic. Migratory species are those whose populations follow regular annual movements between two places. They have separate feeding and breeding habitats, which may be local, within the same country or around the world. Migration is an important part of the breeding cycle.

Many of the birds seen in Australia are trans-equatorial, spending part of the year in the Northern Hemisphere, although migration is less prominent in Australia than in other countries. After breeding, many waders fly to Australia to feed. A number of seabirds breed in Australia and fly north afterwards. The most notable is the Short-tailed Shearwater (*Puffinus tenuirostris*) — after breeding on islands in Bass Strait it migrates to Japan and Siberia and returns via Alaska and the Pacific Ocean.

Many Australian species migrate locally, covering only short distances, usually altitudinally. Others move further afield. At least 50 migrate north-south between the southern mainland and the Top End or New Guinea, the Solomons and Indonesia. Others fly across Bass Strait to Tasmania. Many sub-Antarctic, summer-breeding seabirds spend winter around southern Australia's warmer waters. Few species migrate between Australia and New Zealand. About 25% of Australia's birds are nomadic. Many follow rainfall and food supply across the continent's arid region, breeding only in times of abundance. Others follow the flowering of eucalypt forests or the fruiting of rainforest trees along the east coast.

**Top:** Bar-tailed Godwits migrate to breed in Siberia and Alaska in June and July.

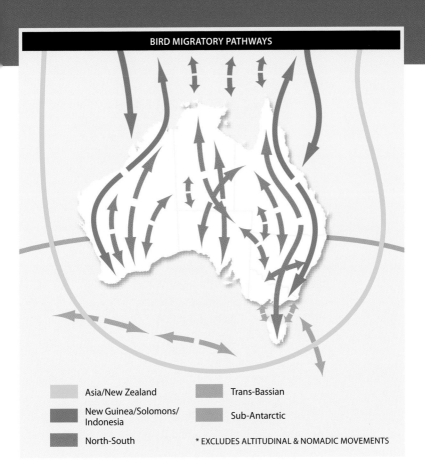

**BIRD MIGRATORY PATHWAYS**

Asia/New Zealand

New Guinea/Solomons/Indonesia

North-South

Trans-Bassian

Sub-Antarctic

* EXCLUDES ALTITUDINAL & NOMADIC MOVEMENTS

## HABITATS & DISTRIBUTION MAPS

Every bird has habitat preferences. Some are more specialised; other more adaptable species inhabit a broad range of habitats. Several habitats may be occupied at different times of the year or in different locations. In transition zones where ecosystems blend into each other, plant diversity increases as does bird life. The vast continent of Australia, ranging across temperate, tropical and arid climatic zones, provides numerous bird habitats.

Erratic rainfall and other weather patterns make it difficult to determine the distributions of many Australian bird species, particularly the nomads. Some areas are consistently inhabited and some, particularly those subject to drought, are only occupied during good seasons. The distribution maps presented throughout this book are drawn from the best field research available.

Gibber plains

Grasslands

Shrublands

Inland water

Woodlands

Closed forests

Open forests

Heathlands

Urban

Dunes

Mangroves

Coastal Islands

# Evolution of Australia's Birds

Piecing together the origins and evolutionary pathways of birds is a challenging science, ever subject to new fossil or DNA evidence. Recognisable birds appeared some 145 million years ago with modern birds emerging only 70–65 million years ago. Opportunities created by the demise of the dinosaurs and the advent of flowering plants stimulated diversification. Over the aeons, continents shifted, carrying their avian cargoes with them. Isolated over time, these developed into different species. Amazingly, in some places the converse occurred. Living in similar habitats on different continents, unrelated birds developed the same features and adaptations.

Today's southern continents were joined for aeons in an enormous land mass referred to as the supercontinent Gondwana, before progressively moving to their present positions. Australia and Antarctica were the last to part, some 45 million years ago. Australia, New Guinea, the Solomon Islands and some of the mid-Pacific islands are on the one continental plate, while New Zealand is on the boundary. Many birds are endemic to this region. Ornithologists, thus recognise Australasia as one of six major geographical regions with distinct bird fauna.

The region's oldest living bird groups include the Emu and cassowaries, mound builders, parrots and possibly the pigeons, cuckoos and rails. With close relatives on other southern continents they are believed to have originated in Gondwana. Recent evidence also suggests that the primitive passerine families originated in and spread throughout Gondwana before moving northwards into Eurasia, and then into North and South America between 85 and 80 million years ago.

**Right:** The Earth 200 million years ago. The black outline indicates the current position of Australia.

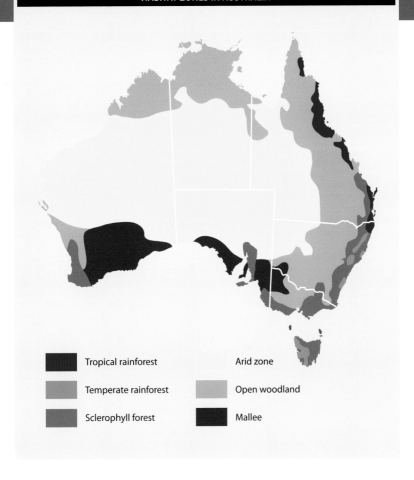

## HABITAT ZONES IN AUSTRALIA

- Tropical rainforest
- Temperate rainforest
- Sclerophyll forest
- Arid zone
- Open woodland
- Mallee

Covered in rainforest for much of its history, Australia dried out as it drifted northwards. Eucalypts and other dry-adapted plants evolved 40–30 million years ago and birds with them. Ice ages and volcanic activity confined rainforests and their bird contingents to eastern mountain refuges. Australia and New Guinea, connected for aeons, separated 10,000 years ago during the last sea level rise. This neighbour shares many Australian species or close relatives.

Australia's bird distributions reflect its habitat zones. Some birds spend their lives in the arid centre. Others live in tropical or temperate regions, in New Guinea or in the mountain rainforest refuges of New Guinea and eastern Australia.

# Emus & Cassowaries

## Order: Struthioniiformes

The Emu, cassowaries, kiwis and Ostrich are flightless birds that probably share a common ancestor dating back to the time of Gondwana. The common ancestor apparently possessed the power of flight, but this ability was lost over time, possibly as a response to a lack of large terrestrial predators. These birds, sometimes known as ratites, lack the keeled sternum and strong flight muscles all other birds possess. Instead they have powerfully built legs and are capable of running at relatively high speeds.

## Southern Cassowary  *Casuarius casuarius*

*Cassowaries are grand birds unique to the Australasian region. The Single-wattled Cassowary (*Casuarius unappendiculatus*) and Dwarf Cassowary (*Casuarius bennetti*) are confined to New Guinea and surrounding islands. The Southern Cassowary lives in New Guinea and north-eastern Australia. The name "cassowary" derives from the Papuan words "kasu", meaning "horned" and "weri" meaning "head".*

**FEATURES:** Cassowaries' coarse, black double-shafted plumage, bright bare necks, large bills, bony helmet-like casques and short, thick scaly legs give them a somewhat prehistoric appearance. The Southern Cassowary has the tallest casque, up to 15 cm high and a double wattle (flap of skin under the neck). Females are larger (average 47 kg; males 38 kg), dominant and have brighter neck colouring.

**DIET & HABITAT:** This mainly frugivorous species forages for fruits, fungi, flowers, snails and other small animals across a mosaic of habitats, including upland and lowland rainforests, swamps and clearings in Far North Queensland.

**BEHAVIOUR & BREEDING:** It is the main disperser of over 70 plant species, many with seeds too large for other animals.

Generally shy and solitary, individuals may be aggressive, particularly if fed by humans. Sexually mature at three years, males and females tolerate each other only during courtship and mating which occurs from July–October. Extremely protective males incubate the large eggs (50 days) and care for the chicks (9–12 months).

**PREDATORS & THREATS:** Defending themselves with strong well-aimed kicks capable of disembowelling pursuers, this species has few predators other than dogs and wild pigs. It is, however, highly vulnerable to extinction through habitat destruction and fragmentation, and collisions with cars.

| | |
|---|---|
| **HEIGHT:** 1.5–1.8 m | **CALL:** Deep booming |
| **NEST:** Scrape on forest floor | **MIGRATION:** Sedentary |
| **EGGS:** 3–5, bright green | **STATUS:** Endangered (Australia); Vulnerable (NG) |

*The endemic Emu is Australia's largest living bird and the world's second largest (after the Ostrich). With a stride of up to 2.5 m it is capable of running at speeds of up to 48 km/h.*

**FEATURES:** The tall, slender long-necked and long-legged Emu has long shaggy grey-brown to black plumage parted down the centre of its back. It has a short, black bill and bare bluish-coloured skin on its head and neck. A short dark feathered crown and a white ruff (plumage at the base of the neck) complete the picture for both sexes.

**DIET & HABITAT:** The Emu ranges across most of mainland Australia's dry open habitats including arid inland plains, semi-arid grasslands, woodlands, heaths, coastal dunes and pastoral areas. Omnivorous, it feeds on a variety of leaves, grasses, fruits, flowers, seeds and insects, depending on the season. It needs to drink regularly, so is usually found within range of water.

The Emu is believed to have evolved from early rainforest-dwelling cassowary ancestors as they adapted to Australia's drying climate. The Tasmanian subspecies (*D. diemenensis*) and two other species (King Island Emu, *D. ater*; Kangaroo Island Emu, *D. baudinianus*) became extinct after European settlement.

**BEHAVIOUR & BREEDING:** The Emu lives in pairs or small "mobs", which may be sedentary or nomadic depending on water and food supply. Females are dominant. In breeding season (April–November), females acquire a dense covering of black feathers over their heads and necks and males' ruffs become more distinct. Mating pairs maintain territories for several months before females lay their clutches in scrapes or trampled vegetation. Males incubate the eggs (53–61 days) and fend for chicks (6–18 months). The chicks' brown and cream striped plumage slowly darkens. They are sexually mature at two years.

**PREDATORS & THREATS:** The Emu is capable of evading most predators, except humans. It has been hunted for food by Aboriginal groups and shot as pests by farmers.

| | |
|---|---|
| **HEIGHT:** 1.5–2 m | **CALL:** Booms |
| **NEST:** Scrape | **MIGRATION:** Sedentary-migratory |
| **EGGS:** 7–11, dark green | **STATUS:** Secure |

# Megapodes
## Order: Galliformes

Megapodes are ground-dwelling game birds that use their strong feet to scratch amongst leaf litter. They have three toes pointing forward and one short hindtoe. These mound builders are unique to Australia, South-East Asia and the South Pacific. They construct large mounds of rotting vegetation and soil and incubate the eggs within them, regulating the temperature by adding or removing material. Australia has three of twelve species. Domestic fowl and popular game birds introduced to Australia, and a few native quails are also included in this group. Native button-quails are similar but unrelated.

**Top:** Orange-footed Scrubfowl.

## Australian Brush-turkey    *Alectura lathami*

*This endemic bird is often seen foraging alone in picnic grounds.*

**DIET & HABITAT:** It lives in rainforest and other dense forests, woodlands and scrubs and feeds on seeds, fruit and invertebrates.

**BEHAVIOUR & BREEDING:** This clumsy flier is usually solitary during the day, however, small groups roost in trees at night. Males' necks and wattles brighten and enlarge during breeding season (August–January). Males maintain the mounds containing the eggs of several females at 35 °C (seven weeks). Dull brown chicks emerge fully independent.

**LENGTH:** 60–70 cm
**NEST:** Mound 1 m x 3 m
**EGGS:** 15–20, white
**CALL:** Grunts, booms
**MIGRATION:** Sedentary
**STATUS:** Secure

## Malleefowl    *Leipoa ocellata*

*This megapode is uniquely adapted to life in arid country.*

**DIET & HABITAT:** It lives amongst mallee and other semi-arid scrublands, eucalypt woodland and coastal heaths. Its diet includes flowers, buds, seeds, fruits and insects.

**BEHAVIOUR & BREEDING:** Adults spend much of their lives preparing for mating. Permanent pairs construct large mounds (autumn). Females lay singular eggs every 2–14 days (September–April). Males maintain mounds at 33 °C (seven weeks). The buff-brown chicks fend for themselves within hours.

**LENGTH:** 55–61 cm
**NEST:** Mound 1.5 m x 2–5 m
**EGGS:** 15–24, pink-brown
**CALL:** Clucks, bellows, croons
**MIGRATION:** Sedentary
**STATUS:** Vulnerable

# Quails & Button-quails

## Order: Galliformes & Order: Turniciformes

Australia has three native species of "true quails". These small, plump ground-dwelling birds have small heads, short legs and small wings. When flushed from long grass they fly with a whirring sound to safety. True quails possess a crop and their feet have three forward-facing toes and a small hindtoe. Button-quails (order: Turnicidae) lack the crop and hindtoe and have reversed gender breeding roles. Australia is home to seven button-quail species out of approximately sixteen worldwide. The Plains-wanderer, also similar, is more closely related to the waders (order: Charadriiformes).

## Stubble Quail  *Coturnix pectoralis*

*Australia's only endemic true quail is seen when flushed out of vegetation during the day, or feeding along road edges at dusk.*

DIET & HABITAT: Living in grasslands, pastures and croplands, it feeds on grass seeds, leaves, insects, frogs, crops and introduced weeds.

BEHAVIOUR & BREEDING: The Stubble Quail may fly long distances to find food, depending on rainfall. Breeding also follows rainfall, generally August–January.

LENGTH: 16–20 cm
NEST: Shallow scrape
EGGS: 6–8, cream
CALL: Piping
MIGRATION: Nomadic
STATUS: Secure

## Painted Button-quail  *Turnix varius*

*This large button-quail rotates while scratching, making circular scrapes in the ground.*

DIET & HABITAT: Habitats include scrubs, heaths and grassy woodlands on rocky hillsides. It feeds on insects, seeds, shoots and berries amongst leaf litter.

BEHAVIOUR & BREEDING: Territorial females call to attract a succession of males, mating each fortnight and laying up to seven clutches per season. Usually males incubate the eggs (two weeks) and rear the chicks (two months).

LENGTH: 17–19 cm
NEST: Depression with canopy
EGGS: 3–4, buff-white
CALL: Drums
MIGRATION: Sedentary-nomadic
STATUS: Secure

# Waterfowl
## Order: Anseriformes

Waterfowl have small heads, buoyant bodies and short tails. Their plumage is waterproof with a layer of down — a layer of fat under the skin provides added insulation. Webbed feet enable powerful swimming or diving. Strong fast fliers, many undertake long migrations. All possess long necks and broad flattened bills for filtering tiny plants and animals from water, seizing aquatic invertebrates, uprooting corms and water plants, grazing on grasses or browsing on seeds and grain. Many form long-term pair bonds. Australia has 25 of the more than 150 worldwide species, with two introduced.

**Top:** The Plumed Whistling-Duck, also known as the Grass Whistling-Duck (*Dendrocygna eytoni*), prefers warmer regions. **Clockwise from top left:** A Blue-billed Duck (*Oxyura australis*); Magpie Geese (*Anseranas semipalmata*) flock; A male Musk Duck (*Biziura lobata*) with breeding accoutrement — an inflatable bill sac; An Australian Wood Duck (*Chenonetta jubata*) leads its ducklings to water; A family of Australian Shelducks (*Tadorna tadornoides*); A male Hardhead (*Aythya australis*) — females have brown eyes.

*The Black Swan, endemic to Australia, is the world's only almost completely black swan. Its elegant shape, musical trumpeting and soft crooning add grace to many coastal and inland waters. Males have deeper voices and their calls are longer, but all swans call to keep in touch.*

**FEATURES:** Australia's largest native waterfowl has the longest neck of all swans — longer than its body. It is suitably regal with predominantly black plumage and white wingtips, a long red bill with white tips and red eyes. The grey cygnets (young swans) turn black at about one year of age.

**DIET & HABITAT:** Tolerating fresh, brackish and salt water it lives over much of Australia, particularly around large permanent swamps and lakes with abundant aquatic vegetation. Introduced to New Zealand, it is plentiful there. The Black Swan dips its long neck up to a metre deep in the water, up-ending when necessary. It tears up bottom-growing plants using the horny hooked nail on its bill tip, or filters small plants via long combs inside the bill. It also grazes on pastures near water.

**BEHAVIOUR & BREEDING:** This swan lives singly or congregates in flocks numbering in the thousands, particularly during moulting. Flocks usually migrate at night in V-shaped formations, flying with their necks outstretched.

Individuals first mate at 2–3 years of age and may choose several mates before pairing permanently, although recent research suggests they may not be faithful partners, as once believed. Pairs construct large mattress nests up to 1 m deep and 3 m wide, on the ground or floating amongst reeds in sheltered waters. Nests may be used several times in a season, by the same pair or others.

Eggs are incubated (39–43 days) by both parents. In the event of neighbouring eggs becoming deserted, pairs move them into their nests and incubate them. Cygnets are raised by both parents. They can swim very quickly but do not fledge until 113–160 days after hatching. While rearing their flightless young, adults moult, becoming flightless themselves.

**PREDATORS & THREATS:** The Black Swan is at its most vulnerable when breeding and moulting and seeks safety in large colonies. Predators include eels, foxes, Dingoes, feral cats and possibly large birds-of-prey.

**LENGTH:** 1.1–1.4 m
**WINGSPAN:** Up to 2 m
**NEST:** Mattress, raft
**EGGS:** 4–6, greenish-white

**CALL:** Bugle, croon
**MIGRATION:** Sedentary-nomadic
**STATUS:** Common

# Plumed Whistling-Duck *Dendrocygna eytoni*

*Australia has three whistling-duck species. None whistle; they are named for the sound their wings create as they fly.*

**DIET & HABITAT:** During the day, groups camp on the ground in wetlands and grasslands. At night they fly to up to 30 km away to feed on grasses, herbs, legumes, rushes and sedges.

**BEHAVIOUR & BREEDING:** Not a strong swimmer or diver, this species is more at home on the land. Parents accompany ducklings to water up to 2 km away.

**LENGTH:** 41–62 cm
**NEST:** Mattress
**EGGS:** 10–12, cream
**CALL:** Whistles, twitters
**MIGRATION:** Migratory
**STATUS:** Secure

# Pacific Black Duck *Anas superciliosa*

*This duck swims within hours of hatching. For its entire short life, it is nomadic, following rainfall across Australia.*

**DIET & HABITAT:** This Australasian species visits permanent and temporary water bodies but prefers deep freshwater swamps. It feeds on seeds and a wide range of aquatic invertebrates.

**BEHAVIOUR & BREEDING:** Breeding after rain when food is plentiful, females raise ducklings alone, with short outings on the water. At 8–10 weeks young fly off to join small flocks.

**LENGTH:** 48–60 cm
**NEST:** Various
**EGGS:** 8–10, green-white
**CALL:** Quacks, peeps
**MIGRATION:** Nomadic
**STATUS:** Secure

# Grey Teal *Anas gracilis*

*The Grey Teal, Australia's most widespread duck, is at home on any water body.*

**DIET & HABITAT:** This dabbling duck is most abundant around tree-lined, inland billabongs. It feeds on seeds and a range of aquatic invertebrates.

**BEHAVIOUR & BREEDING:** Highly nomadic, flocks wander the country in search of water and food, congregating around permanent coastal wetlands during drought. Pairs breed in inland waters after rain. Most birds survive for only 1–2 years.

**LENGTH:** 40–46 cm
**NEST:** Various, near water
**EGGS:** 7–8, cream
**CALL:** Quacks, peeps
**MIGRATION:** Dispersive
**STATUS:** Secure

# Australian Shelduck  *Tadorna tadornoides*

*After breeding, this large duck migrates long distances to moult in safety.*

**DIET & HABITAT:** Large, shallow water bodies; fresh, brackish or saline are preferred. Shelducks graze on grasses and sedges and dabble or upend for aquatic invertebrates and plants. They also sift muddy water or mudflats.

**BEHAVIOUR & BREEDING:** Flocks fly in V-shaped formations or wavering lines. Permanent pairs rest during the day in family parties or large flocks. Both sexes rear the chicks.

**LENGTH:** 55–74 cm
**NEST:** Hollow, scrape
**EGGS:** 8–14, cream
**CALL:** Sizzing grunts
**MIGRATION:** Local migrant
**STATUS:** Secure

---

# Green Pygmy-goose  *Nettapus pulchellus*

*Australia is home to two of the world's three pygmy-geese. These tropical waterfowl are in fact small perching ducks.*

**DIET & HABITAT:** They are found around Australia's vegetated tropical water bodies, where they upend water plants and graze on seeds. In the wet season, the Green Pygmy-goose disperses to shallow swamps — in the dry it congregates on permanent waters.

**BEHAVIOUR & BREEDING:** Both species spend most of their time on water and breed during wetter months.

**LENGTH:** 4–38 cm
**NEST:** Hollow near water
**EGGS:** 6–10, creamy-white
**CALL:** Trills
**MIGRATION:** Sedentary
**STATUS:** Secure

---

# Australian Wood Duck  *Chenonetta jubata*

*Also known as the Maned Goose, this bird is more often seen on the ground or perched in a tree, than in the water.*

**DIET & HABITAT:** It prefers lightly timbered grasslands near water. Family groups camp during the day in flocks of 100–2000, and feed at night on seeds, sedges, herbs and grass shoots.

**BEHAVIOUR & BREEDING:** This nomadic duck has shorter, more regular movements than other inland ducks. Females coax ducklings from the nest high in a tree hollow and lead them to water.

**LENGTH:** 44–50 cm
**NEST:** Hollow near water
**EGGS:** 9–12, creamy-white
**CALL:** Mewing, clucking
**MIGRATION:** Sedentary-nomadic
**STATUS:** Secure

# Cape Barren Goose  *Cereopsis novaehollandiae*

*Little understood for many years, the robust Cape Barren Goose is now believed to be an intermediate between a goose and a duck.*

**DIET & HABITAT:** It breeds on small, remote and uninhabited islands from autumn to winter, and then grazes on pasture on larger inshore islands during early summer. Preferred foods include tussock grass, spear grass, herbs and succulent plants. Well-developed salt excretion glands allow it to survive on salt or brackish water for most of the year.

**LENGTH:** 75–100 cm
**NEST:** Mattress
**EGGS:** 4–5, lustrous white
**CALL:** Honks, grunts
**MIGRATION:** Local migrant
**STATUS:** Secure

**BEHAVIOUR & BREEDING:** Males aggressively guard incubating females (34–37 days) and share the parenting (4–6 weeks). Young join nomadic flocks (50–250), mating at about three years.

**PREDATORS & THREATS:** It is one of the world's rarest fowl. On the brink of extinction in the 1950s, its future is now secure.

# Magpie Goose  *Anseranas semipalmata*

*The Magpie Goose lives only in Australia and New Guinea. Not a true goose, it has only partially webbed feet, enabling it to perch. Older individuals, particularly males, bear a distinctive knob on their heads.*

**DIET & HABITAT:** Vocal flocks roost around seasonal and permanent coastal waterholes. In the dry season family groups range further inland. This species grazes on swamp grass seeds and spike-rush bulbs.

**LENGTH:** 71–92 cm
**NEST:** Floating mound 1.5 m x 0.5 m
**EGGS:** 6–8/female, creamy-white
**CALL:** Honks, whistles
**MIGRATION:** Mostly sedentary
**STATUS:** Secure

**BEHAVIOUR & BREEDING:** During the wet season, breeding pairs or trios (one male with two females) share incubation and rearing duties. At eleven weeks, young can fly; together with their parents they join other family groups to form loose flocks.

**PREDATORS & THREATS:** The main predator is the Dingo, with other threats being shooting, habitat destruction and drought.

# Grebes
## Order: Podicipediformes

Grebes are waterbirds especially adapted for diving and swimming underwater, with lobed feet for propulsion and dense water-resistant plumage. Despite short stubby wings, they fly long distances between habitats, often at night. Three of the world's twenty species live in Australia's inland ponds and lakes. Generally fish-eaters, some also eat snails, tadpoles, insect larvae, crustaceans and aquatic plants. All eat their own feathers and sometimes feed them to their young. This may prevent internal puncture wounds from fish bones or help with the regurgitation of indigestible scales and bones.

**Right:** Great Crested Grebe (*Podiceps cristatus*).

## Australasian Grebe *Tachybaptus novaehollandiae*

**FEATURES:** Breeding plumage is vastly different from its usual nondescript fawn-grey-brown. This grebe's neck and breast darken and the head is black with a chestnut neck-stripe and a small yellow patch at the bill base. Eyes are yellow.

**DIET & HABITAT:** It prefers smaller water bodies such as farm dams, lakes and swamps. It feeds on the surface or in the shallows, diving often for small fish, snails and the like.

**BEHAVIOUR & BREEDING:** Monogamous pairs share parental duties (August–December). The floating nests are usually attached to reeds and the eggs are often wet. Young are sometimes carried under parents' wings, even when they dive.

**PREDATORS & THREATS:** When predators approach the nest, the parent on incubation duty simply pulls nest materials over the eggs and slips into the water, resurfacing some distance away.

*Living throughout Australasia, this grebe also finds suitable, usually freshwater, habitat across much of Australia.*

**LENGTH:** 23–26 cm
**NEST:** Floating raft
**EGGS:** 4–5, bluish-white

**CALL:** Chitter, trill
**MIGRATION:** Sedentary-nomadic
**STATUS:** Secure

# Penguins

## Order: Sphenisciformes

Penguins are believed to have descended from petrel-like ancestors. Now flightless, with solid wings adapted as flippers, they spend their lives in or near the world's southern oceans. Their streamlined bodies are insulated by waterproofed feathers and down and a layer of blubber under the skin. Solid bones reduce buoyancy. Counter-shaded plumage provides camouflage. Penguins moult and breed annually, on shore. Eleven of eighteen species occur in Australian waters, mostly on Antarctica or around sub-Antarctic islands. Only one breeds on Australian shores.

**Top:** The Little Penguin (*Eudyptula minor*) — Australia's only true resident penguin.
**Clockwise from top left:** Fjordland Penguin (*Eudyptes pachyrhynchus*) at home in the water and on land; The Fjordland Penguin breeds in NZ only and occasionally comes ashore to moult on Australian coasts; The King Penguin (*Aptenodytes patagonicus*) is one of the larger penguins. It breeds on Australian sub-Antarctic territory of Macquarie and Heard Islands and is a vagrant to Australia's coastline; Little Penguins come ashore in small "rafts" or groups.

*Standing a mere 45 cm tall and weighing only 1 kg, this diminutive penguin is well named — it is the smallest in the world. Also known as the Fairy Penguin, it is the only species that lives and breeds in Australia, and is also found around New Zealand. Breeding colonies in southern Australia are popular ecotourist attractions at night. Visitors can watch large numbers of adults as they come ashore, make their way to their nests and greet their young.*

**FEATURES:** The plumage often takes a bluish sheen. Flippers are used to "fly" underwater. Large eyes provide excellent vision, both underwater and on land. Claws on the webbed feet are used for digging burrows and climbing up slippery shores.

**DIET & HABITAT:** This species spends autumn and winter at sea. It feeds alone or in small groups on small school fish, squid and krill, which it swallows whole with the assistance of numerous barbs inside its long beak. It may herd and charge shoals of fish or dive for prey, often to between 10–30 m, but occasionally up to 60 m. Its scientific name, *Eudyptula*, means "good little diver".

**BEHAVIOUR & BREEDING:** The Little Penguin is highly vocal and one of few penguin species active after dark. It comes ashore only to breed along the southern coastline of Australia (August–February in Victoria and Tasmania; April–December in Western Australia). Males arrive first to renovate old nests or build new ones in sand dunes or rocky areas up to 200 m from the ocean shore. They attract females with noisy displays. Pairs share parental duties, incubating eggs for five weeks and then alternating chick-sitting and feeding duties for about two weeks. The feeding parent departs at dawn and returns after dusk, regurgitating food for the chicks. From two weeks both parents fish all day to feed the rapidly growing chicks, which are by then old enough to fend for themselves. Chicks are independent and move to the sea at 7–8 weeks. Most survive to this stage but only 15% survive to breeding age (two years). A lucky few live to six years of age.

**PREDATORS & THREATS:** Water rats, quolls, seagulls, ravens and the White-bellied Sea-Eagle all prey on Little Penguin chicks or adults while they are on land. In the sea, Leopard Seals, fur-seals and sharks are formidable predators. Feral animals and habitat destruction add to this species' naturally high mortality rate.

**LENGTH:** 40–45 cm

**NEST:** Tunnel (60–80 cm long), cave, crevice

**EGGS:** 2, white-pale blue

**CALL:** Yap, bray, growl, mew

**MIGRATION:** Dispersive

**STATUS:** Secure

# Tube-nosed Seabirds

## Order: Procellariiformes

Most of this group of wide-ranging ocean birds (approximately 100 species) possess two nostrils that meet in a tube on the top of the hooked bill — keeping saltwater out of their noses when they dive. An unusually strong sense of smell allows them to locate schools of fish, plankton and breeding islands at night. They come ashore only to breed. Their front toes are webbed and the hindtoe is small or absent. They excrete excess salt through glands near their eyes. Generally mating for life, they invest heavily in successive single offspring.

## Shy Albatross  *Diomedea cauta*

*The largest of the tube-nosed seabirds are the albatrosses. Of the world's 24 species, most breed in the Southern Hemisphere, four of them on sub-Antarctic Macquarie Island. Only the Shy Albatross breeds in Tasmania.*

**FEATURES:** The counter-shaded Shy Albatross has a white crown that forms a distinctive cap over its grey brows and dark eyes. The grey bill has a pale yellow tip, and, as in other albatross species, the top mandible overhangs the bottom; this allows it to hold its prey. Its webbed feet are blue-grey. Subspecies (*T. c. cauta*, *T. c. salvini*, *T. c. eremita*) differ slightly.

**DIET & HABITAT:** This albatross generally feeds in relatively shallow waters close to the edge of the continental shelf. It captures small fish and squid at the ocean surface, occasionally diving to over 7 m.

**BEHAVIOUR & BREEDING:** The Shy Albatross breeds annually on Albatross Island (5000 pairs), Pedra Branca (200–250 pairs) and The Mewstone (over 7000 pairs), three tiny rock islands off Tasmania's coastline. Pairs claim nesting sites amongst the crowded colonies (June–July) before laying (August) and incubating eggs (November–December), then rearing nestbound chicks (until April–

May). Mortality rates are high and adults have little time to prepare before breeding again. Young take to the skies, returning two years later to learn about courting and nesting.

**PREDATORS & THREATS:** Because albatrosses reach sexual maturity late, reproduce via single-egg clutches and experience low breeding success, they are vulnerable to human impacts. Long-line tuna fishing in the Southern Ocean continues to be their greatest threat.

| | |
|---|---|
| **LENGTH:** 90–100 cm | **EGGS:** 1, white |
| **WEIGHT:** 3.4–4.4 kg | **MIGRATION:** Dispersive |
| **WINGSPAN:** 2.1–2.6 m | **STATUS:** Vulnerable (Australia) |
| **NEST:** Scrape, bowl | |

Ten species of shearwaters or "muttonbirds" spend part of the year along Australian coastlines. One of the most commonly encountered, the Wedge-tailed Shearwater, is responsible for the wailing sounds heard at night on Great Barrier Reef islands.

**FEATURES:** All shearwaters are strong fliers with small lightweight bodies and large wingspans. This species is distinguished by its broad wings, which it holds well forward, its long wedge-shaped tail, dark grey bill and flesh-coloured feet. It has two colour morphs, one grey all over and the other dark above and mostly white below.

**DIET & HABITAT:** The Wedge-tailed Shearwater inhabits Australia's warmer coastal waters, breeding on inshore islands. It also ranges across the tropical Pacific and Indian Oceans. Like other shearwaters, it commonly plunges up to 14 m deep in pursuit of open-ocean fish, squid and crustaceans. It also snatches prey from the ocean surface and follows trawlers. Its hooked beak helps it hold its prey.

**BEHAVIOUR & BREEDING:** Shearwaters are named for their habit of gliding gracefully just above the ocean surface. This species has a particularly gentle and buoyant flight pattern.

Like other shearwaters, it breeds in crowded colonies (October–May) from the age of 4–5 years. Pair bonds last several breeding seasons if breeding is successful; these bonds appear to be reinforced by calling together. Nests are constructed in 1–2 m long burrows in sand dunes, or in crevices or logs. Males and females alternate incubation shifts (up to thirteen days, for a total of 50 days). Chicks are brooded until their body temperatures stabilise (six days). Both parents then hunt for food, returning regularly. After 103–115 days, chicks fledge and become independent.

**PREDATORS & THREATS:** Although abundant, shearwaters suffer from the effects of human activities, including uncontrolled hunting. Grazing livestock and soil erosion can destroy burrows, even whole colonies. Predation by feral cats and swallowing plastic can be fatal.

**Top:** The nostrils of the Wedge-tailed Shearwater and other tube-nosed seabirds are distinctive.  **Inset:** A nesting pair inside their burrow.

| | |
|---|---|
| **LENGTH:** 38–46 cm | **EGGS:** Single, white |
| **WINGSPAN:** 1 m | **CALL:** Wailing |
| **NEST:** 1–2 m burrow, crevices, logs | **MIGRATION:** Part migratory |
| | **STATUS:** Secure |

# Pelicans & Other Seabirds

## Order: Pelecaniformes

These seabirds are the only birds that possess webbing on all four toes. They are very strong swimmers with huge feet, compact waterproof plumage and small or closed nostrils. They inhabit the world's oceans and some inland waters. Many mate for life, devoting considerable energy to courtship displays, and caring for naked chicks for prolonged periods. Seventeen of the world's 65 species live in Australia.

Pelicans (family: Pelecanidae, seven species) are the best known. They feed, often cooperatively, by herding and scooping fish, crustaceans, frogs, insects and sometimes ducklings into their expandable bill pouches. The Australian Pelican (*Pelecanus conspicillatus*) is Australia's only pelican and largest flying bird, with a wingspan of over 2.5 m and weighing up to 8.2 kg. Capable of soaring on thermals to heights of 3 km, it makes long distance migrations and precision landings.

Gannets and boobies (family: Sulidae) have large strong bills that merge into a mask around their eyes and sealed nostrils. These strong-flying precision-hunters wheel over the ocean in large flocks, herding fish before plunge-diving from 20–30 m in the air, at speeds of up to 95 km/h. Extra air spaces beneath their skin absorb the shock. Swallowing fish underwater, these birds quickly return to the air.

**Top:** Grace in-flight — the Australian Pelican. **Right:** The Australasian Gannet (*Morus serrator*) breeds in noisy colonies. The nest is a mound of vegetation and guano.

**Clockwise from top left:** The male Brown Booby (*Sula leucogaster*) has a blue face; The usually solitary Red-tailed Tropicbird (*Phaethon rubricauda*) complete with "tail streamers"; A Darter (*Anhinga melanogaster*) warming its wings in the sun; Pelicans are quick to exploit feeding opportunities. They often feed in flocks.

The lesser-known tropicbirds (family: Phaethontidae) feed in the same way. These elegant birds resemble large terns but have long colourful tail plumes. In contrast, frigatebirds (family: Fregatidae) feed by snatching fish from the surface or from other seabirds. They have long hooked beaks and forked tails. Males vastly inflate their bright red throat pouches during courtship displays.

Darters (family: Anhingidae) and cormorants (family: Phalacrocoracidae) dive for food. Adaptations for diving include bones without air spaces, saturated outer feathers to reduce buoyancy, waterproof inner feathers, sealed nostrils and the habit of swallowing stones. Cormorants chase quarry underwater, and darters wait in ambush and spear prey quickly.

# Herons & Their Relatives

## Order: Ciconiiformes

Twenty of the world's 115 species of large bodied, long-legged waders are commonly seen around Australian wetlands, pastures and grasslands. Using their long heavy bills and a range of inventive strategies they hunt fish, amphibians, small reptiles and mammals and various invertebrates. Most roost and nest in treetop colonies, often with each other and other species including cormorants and gulls. Their loose plumage is enhanced by breeding colours and plumes. Monogamous, both sexes care for the helpless chicks. Like passerines, they have three forward toes and one hindtoe.

## Herons, Egrets & Bitterns    Family: Ardeidae

Herons and egrets are medium to tall slender wading birds with long necks and legs; bitterns are smaller. Skilled and solitary hunters, they wade, stand still in ambush or stir up prey with one foot, then thrust their long, straight sharp bills into the water to spear their victims. Prey, including a variety of aquatic vertebrates and invertebrates, are gripped tightly between the finely serrated bill edges before being swallowed. Specialised vertebrae allow sudden straightening and thrusting of the neck.

Easily recognisable in-flight, their long necks coil into an S shape and their long legs trail behind. Plumage varies. Three of Australia's five egrets are all white even when bearing long, wispy breeding plumage; their bills and bare skin change colour instead. The Cattle Egret (*Ardea ibis*) bears striking breeding plumage. The Eastern Reef Egret (*Egretta sacra*) has both a white and dark grey form. Five herons are largely grey but the nocturnal Nankeen Night Heron (*Nycticorax caledonicus*) has predominantly chestnut plumage. The reclusive and usually partially nocturnal bitterns (four species) are chestnut, black or cryptic. Relying on camouflage they often freeze with their bills pointing upwards. Most herons and bitterns produce powder down which is spread through the plumage after cleaning the feathers with the serrated nail on their middle toes.

Fourteen of the world's 62 species in this family live in Australia. The largest is the Great-billed Heron (*Ardea sumatrana*, 1.2 m long from bill to tail); the smallest is the Little Bittern (*Ixobrychus minutus*, 25–35 cm long).

**Left:** The male Cattle Egret (*Ardea ibis*) has wispy breeding plumes (top). The female (bottom) lays one to two eggs on a flimsy stick platform. Pairs breed in loose colonies.

**Clockwise from top:** A graceful Great Egret (*Ardea alba*) hunting in a shallow lagoon. The largest of the egrets, it lives around the coast and much of inland Australia; The distinctive Pied Heron (*Ardea picata*) is a tropical-dweller, found only around the coastal swamps and grasslands of the Top End; Cattle Egret (*Ardea ibis*) in breeding plumage; A White-faced Heron (*Egretta novaehollandiae*) tending its nest. This species lives throughout most of Australia.

Ibises and spoonbills are medium to large long-legged freshwater waders. Ibises have long thin curved bills for probing and withdrawing prey from mud or water. Spoonbills are easily recognised by their straight bills widened at the tip like spoons. They usually swish these back and forth through water and locate prey by touch. Both groups also feed in dry grasslands. Prey includes frogs, snakes, insects, crustaceans, fish and molluscs.

Despite their differently shaped bills, ibises and spoonbills are closely related and share many similarities. Both groups have bare skin on their faces and/or necks. They are all highly gregarious, roosting and nesting in extremely large flocks, which are exceptionally noisy despite these birds' lack of a voice box. Both groups communicate in grunts or croaks and spoonbills clap their bills together. When travelling, flocks fly in V formations with their long necks extended and legs trailing behind.

Of the world's 26 ibis species, three occur in Australia — the Glossy (*Plegadis falcinellus*), Straw-necked (*Threskiornis spinicollis*) and Australian White Ibis (*Threskiornis molucca*). Extremely adaptable, they are all widespread across the country's less arid regions. As ibises often forage for leaf-eating insects such as grasshoppers, consuming up to 25% of their body weight every day, they are often considered to be "farmers' friends". Courting and nesting ibises are recognised by their ritual bowing ceremonies. Breeding pairs preen each other.

Two of the five spoonbill species in Australia are native; the Yellow-billed Spoonbill (*Platalea flavipes*) is endemic. Less common but more striking is the Royal Spoonbill (*Platalea regia*). During breeding season its dark bill and face are framed by glorious white plumes about 15 cm long on the nape of its neck. These are raised whenever other birds approach.

In breeding season, Yellow-billed Spoonbills also grow long white display plumes, from just above their breasts. Males are extremely aggressive during this period.

**Top:** The Royal Spoonbill (*Platalea regia*) is a striking bird, particularly in breeding season. **Right:** The Australian White Ibis (*Threskiornis molucca*). Courting males display on tree branches.

*Storks are the largest of the freshwater wading birds. In many parts of the world they are considered good omens. The Black-necked Stork is Australia's only member of the stork family (Ciconiidae, seventeen species) and more commonly known as the Jabiru (a Brazilian not Aboriginal name as many suppose).*

**FEATURES:** Like most other storks it has distinctive pied plumage (in this case glossy green-black and white), brightly coloured legs and a very long robust bill. It is one of the larger storks and definitely one of Australia's largest birds (wingspan up to 2.2 m).

**DIET & HABITAT:** It lives around freshwater swamps, lakes, estuaries, lagoons and tidal flats in northern and eastern Australia, but is most common across the Top End. It also inhabits wetlands through New Guinea and South-East Asia to India. Generally hunting alone it usually stalks its prey — crustaceans, amphibians, small mammals and reptiles — and chases them with leaping strides before thrusting its bill forward to catch them. It also eats insects and carrion.

**BEHAVIOUR & BREEDING:** This stork is sometimes seen in pairs or small family groups. Although it needs to take a series of running jumps to get airborne, it is capable of soaring long distances. Like other storks, it flies with its neck and legs extended. Believed mute, adults clap their bills, mainly at the nest.

During breeding season (March–June in the north, August–April in the south) pairs share nest building, incubation and brooding duties. The nest is a dry grass mattress on top of a large stick platform, usually constructed on a stump, on top of a small tree or in a fork high in a tall tree near water. In hot weather, parents regurgitate water over the eggs and brown chicks to keep them cool. Young leave the nest at 100–115 days.

**PREDATORS & THREATS:** Destruction of wetlands and water pollution have reduced the Black-necked Stork's range. Nestlings deter predators by lifting their wings and clattering their bills.

**Top:** Females have yellow eyes; males' eyes are brown.  **Above:** A rare sight — a courting pair.

**HEIGHT:** 1.4 m
**NEST:** Mattress on platform
**EGGS:** 3, white

**CALL:** Claps bill
**MIGRATION:** Nomadic
**STATUS:** Secure

# Raptors
## Order: Falconiformes

Australia is home to 24 of the world's total species of diurnal birds-of-prey, often referred to as raptors. These agile hunting birds are characterised by strong muscular legs and taloned feet for capturing prey and sharp hooked bills for tearing them apart. Acute binocular vision and excellent hearing enable them to locate prey; large powerful wings enable circling and soaring, and swooping or diving in ambush. As they fly the feathers on their wingtips separate, increasing stability. They hunt a wide range of vertebrates and invertebrates and sometimes eat carrion. Females are usually larger than males. All are monogamous, maintaining long-term territories and reusing nests (generally large stick platforms) for numerous years. Many living in Australia also range widely overseas; seven are endemic.

The Osprey (*Pandion haliaetus*) and most eagles, hawks and harriers (family: Accipitridae) kill their prey by piercing vital organs and breaking bones with their talons, but some also deliver a fatal bite. The fast and acrobatic falcons and kestrels (family: Falconidae) pursue and kill their prey (smaller birds), usually on the wing, via a strong kick or by biting through the vertebral column at the base of the skull with the purpose-designed "tooth" on the edge of their beaks. Raptors regurgitate indigestible remains including bones, feathers and fur. Other birds exhibit nervous or alarmed behaviour whenever raptors are near.

**Top:** A powerful bill makes the Wedge-tailed Eagle (*Aquila audax*) a ferocious predator. **Right:** The Peregrine Falcon (*Falco peregrinus*) has keen eyesight.

## Osprey  *Pandion haliaetus*

*This large graceful hunter patrols 10–50 m above water, plunging and submerging feet first before flying off with fish in its talons. Talons are equipped with spiny scales and a reversible outer front toe.*

**DIET & HABITAT:** Widely distributed overseas, in Australia the Osprey lives around coastal and occasionally inland waters, perching on posts and cliff faces, hunting fish and sometimes sea snakes.

**BEHAVIOUR & BREEDING:** Courting males pursue females in acrobatic plunge-dives.

**LENGTH:** 50–65 cm
**WINGSPAN:** 1.7 m
**NEST:** Sticks, driftwood
**EGGS:** 2, white & brown
**CALL:** Plaintive "pseek-pseek"
**MIGRATION:** Sedentary
**STATUS:** Secure

# Whistling Kite  *Haliastur sphenurus*

*This large kite calls in a descending whistle while soaring with slow wingbeats or gliding effortlessly with its wings bowed upwards.*

**DIET & HABITAT:** It prefers open forests and woodlands near swamps, rivers, lakes or the coast. It scavenges all manner of carrion, occasionally hunting waterbirds, water rats, freshwater crayfish and insects.

**BEHAVIOUR & BREEDING:** The Whistling Kite is usually seen alone, in pairs or in small travelling groups.

**LENGTH:** 50–60 cm
**WINGSPAN:** 1.2 m
**NEST:** Stick platform
**EGGS:** 2, dull white
**CALL:** Shrill whistle
**MIGRATION:** Sedentary-nomadic
**STATUS:** Secure

# Pacific Baza  *Aviceda subcristata*

*Also known as the Crested Hawk for its prominent crest, this raptor hunts in the treetops by plunging into the foliage in pursuit of small prey.*

**DIET & HABITAT:** Mainly insectivorous it also eats reptiles, frogs and small mammals, which it hunts while hanging upside down or via acrobatic manoeuvres through the air. It prefers woodlands and forests along watercourses.

**BEHAVIOUR & BREEDING:** Courting birds engage in spectacular aerial displays.

**LENGTH:** 36–45 cm
**WINGSPAN:** 80 cm
**NEST:** Saucer, on mistletoe
**EGGS:** 2–4, blue-white
**CALL:** Short trills
**MIGRATION:** Sedentary
**STATUS:** Secure

# Spotted Harrier  *Circus assimilis*

*With acute hearing the Spotted Harrier glides slowly low over grasslands and crops, flushing out prey. Although killed on the ground, prey is eaten on a perch.*

**DIET & HABITAT:** It inhabits drier grasslands and woodlands leaving the wetter areas to the Swamp Harrier (*Circus approximans*). It squeals shrilly while attacking insects, small reptiles, birds and mammals.

**BEHAVIOUR & BREEDING:** Courting males soar to great heights, descending in slow spirals or sideways slips.

**LENGTH:** 50–61 cm
**WINGSPAN:** 1.2 m
**NEST:** Stick platform
**EGGS:** 3, pale blue-white
**CALL:** Usually silent
**MIGRATION:** Sedentary-part migratory
**STATUS:** Secure

# White-bellied Sea-Eagle   *Haliaeetus leucogaster*

*This majestic eagle glides gracefully on long broad wings held in a V, or soars to great heights using slow powerful wingbeats. It patrols high over land or sea and swoops to snatch prey from the surface with its powerful talons but seldom enters water.*

**DIET & HABITAT:** This large eagle is found along the coastline of Australia and around inland lakes and rivers. It skilfully hunts a wide variety of prey including fish, reptiles, birds, mammals, tideline offal and carrion, and harries the Osprey and terns for theirs.

**BEHAVIOUR & BREEDING:** Pairs raise single chicks annually; females do most of the incubation and brooding. Chicks stay with their parents for a few months after learning to fly.

**PREDATORS & THREATS:** Removal of nesting sites and urban development impact on numbers.

**LENGTH:** 70–90 cm

**WINGSPAN:** Up to 2 m

**NEST:** Huge stick nes with view over water

**EGGS:** 2, dull white

**CALL:** Metallic clanking, duets

**MIGRATION:** Sedentary-dispersive

**STATUS:** Secure

# Wedge-tailed Eagle   *Aquila audax*

*Australia's largest eagle is an aerial performer! Courting pairs circle high, then fold their wings and dive. Males may dive at females which then roll over in midair to present their talons. However, a pair locking claws and tumbling usually represents a territorial dispute.*

**DIET & HABITAT:** This eagle lives across Australia in all habitats, except rainforest. It scavenges and hunts large wildlife, particularly kangaroos, wallabies, rabbits and some reptiles.

**BEHAVIOUR & BREEDING:** With a wingspan of up to 2.8 m, it is capable of soaring for hours and can reach dizzying heights — up to 2 km. Breeding pairs often maintain 2–3 nests as feeding stations. The stronger nestling usually kills the weaker.

**PREDATORS & THREATS:** This eagle is vulnerable to pesticides. It is slow to take flight when feeding on roadkill.

**LENGTH:** 90–110 cm

**WINGSPAN:** Up to 2.8 m

**NEST:** Huge stick nes with commanding view

**EGGS:** 2, white and brown

**CALL:** High-pitched "pseet-you"

**MIGRATION:** Sedentary-nomadic

**STATUS:** Endangered in Tasmania

# Peregrine Falcon *Falco peregrinus*

*The Peregrine Falcon is the ultimate speedster, the fastest bird on Earth, capable of diving at over 200 km/h. It attacks other birds in a spectacular swooping dive, catching them in its talons or striking with its foot to knock them to the ground.*

**LENGTH:** 36–47 cm
**WINGSPAN:** Up to 95 cm
**NEST:** Various
**EGGS:** 3, pink-white
**CALL:** Loud screams
**MIGRATION:** Sedentary
**STATUS:** Secure

**DIET & HABITAT:** Australian habitats include woodlands, wetlands, cliffs and even cities. Other birds, including pigeons, parrots, starlings and ducks, fall prey to this hunter. Its presence creates panic amongst potential victims.

**BEHAVIOUR & BREEDING:** Courting birds engage in noisy aerial manoeuvres. Pairs frequently nest on ledges or cliff faces.

**PREDATORS & THREATS:** This living emblem of falconry is slowly recovering from the effects of DDT poisoning during the 1950s and 1960s in Europe and the USA.

# Brown Falcon *Falco berigora*

*Unlike most other falcons, this bird flies with slow wingbeats, or glides with wings held in a shallow V. It swoops down to grasp prey in its talons or chases it on the ground. Several forms, dark brown to light red-brown, occur in Australia.*

**LENGTH:** 40–50 cm
**WINGSPAN:** 1.2 m
**NEST:** Unused nest
**EGGS:** 3, buff-red-brown
**CALL:** Cackles, chuckles, screeches
**MIGRATION:** Sedentary-nomadic
**STATUS:** Secure

**DIET & HABITAT:** Preferring more open country, the Brown Falcon is found throughout Australia, except in rainforests. It hunts small mammals, birds, reptiles and invertebrates, particularly grasshoppers.

**BEHAVIOUR & BREEDING:** Courtship displays include circling, spectacular dives and gliding with wings in a shallow V, all accompanied by loud cackling.

**PREDATORS & THREATS:** The Brown Falcon has coarser scales than other Australian falcons on its legs; these serve as armour against snakebite.

# Cranes, Rails, Coots, Bustards & Relatives

## Order: Gruiformes

Nineteen of some 180 species of ground-feeding birds with long legs and feet adapted for wading or walking occur in Australia. They are grouped into three families — family: Gruidae, the cranes; family: Rallidae, the abundant and diverse rail family; and family: Otididae, the bustards. Although diverse in size and shape, they share similar features of internal anatomy such as lacking a crop.

The long-legged cranes have long toes to distribute their weight, slender bills and rounded wings. Many species migrate long distances to their remote wetland breeding habitats, congregating at long-established stop-overs. Their trumpeting calls are amplified by incredibly long windpipes, coiled within their chests. Mating for life, cranes are famous for their elaborate courtship rituals, including elegant dances. Australia has two crane species.

Rails, crakes and gallinules are small to medium sized waterbirds, the gallinules possessing coloured bills and forehead shields. They hunt amongst low vegetation and reeds by walking, wading or swimming. When alarmed they flick their tails and run over the ground or across the water surface flapping their wings. Rails attract mates via loud calls and elegant displays. These shy birds nest on the ground or amongst reeds in pairs or breeding groups. A few are flightless, but many are nomadic, found worldwide. Australia has sixteen species.

The Australian Bustard (*Ardeotis australis*) is one of 24 bustard species worldwide, found in grasslands and plains. These large long-necked and stately birds hold their heads tilted backwards as they walk. With strong legs and short toes, they are fast runners; relying on their camouflage, they fly only when in serious danger. Males inflate their throat sacs, fan their tails and call loudly to attract mates. Females raise young alone.

This group is disproportionately endangered by human activities particularly habitat destruction, hunting and the introduction of ground predators. Seven of the world's fourteen crane species are endangered. International cooperation is required to protect breeding wetlands and migration stop-overs.

**Top:** The Tasmanian Native-hen (*Gallinula mortierii*) lives only in Tasmania. **Right:** Buff-banded Rail (*Gallirallus philippensis*).

# Brolga  *Grus rubicunda*

*The Brolga is the more widespread and common of Australia's two native cranes; the other is the Sarus Crane (*Grus antigone*). Large flocks of up to 12,000 individuals have been seen at more permanent wetlands (including Kakadu, Cape York, Atherton Tableland and Townsville Town Common) during drier months.*

**FEATURES:** The Brolga is pale grey with dark flight feathers and legs and a small red patch on its head. The Sarus Crane has a larger red patch on its head and neck, and only its wingtips are dark. Brolga chicks are grey — Sarus Crane chicks are brown.

**DIET & HABITAT:** The Brolga usually lives around shallow freshwater wetlands dominated by sedges in north-eastern Australia and New Guinea. While wading in the shallows it digs for sedge tubers with its head underwater. It also feeds on insects and seeds in grasslands, croplands and claypans.

**BEHAVIOUR & BREEDING:** This elegant species flies with slow wingbeats, with its long neck and legs extended. Pairs breed near water during the wet season (September–June in the north, July–March in the south) after elaborate courtship "dances". Pairs face each other, step forward with wings open, bob and bow, retire and leap into the air, as well as toss pieces of grass and twigs around. Pairs share incubation, brooding and guard duties for up to eleven months. Nests are dry grass mattresses on the ground or in the shallows. Chicks are able to run and swim early on, but require feeding and protection.

After breeding, large numbers congregate around wetlands (away from breeding areas) where pairs trumpet in duet and dance to strengthen their permanent bonds. The Brolga also trumpets in-flight.

**PREDATORS & THREATS:** The drainage and reclamation of wetlands for agriculture and urban development combined with overgrazing, weeds and introduced ground predators have limited the Brolga's range.

**Top:** A Brolga dancing.  **Inset:** A flock in-flight — a sight to behold.

**HEIGHT:** 70 cm–1.3 m
**WINGSPAN:** 1.7–2.4 m
**NEST:** Grass mattress
**EGGS:** 2, white-red-brown

**CALL:** Trumpets, duets
**MIGRATION:** Local migrant-dispersive
**STATUS:** Secure

# Waders

## Order: Charadriiformes

About 350 diverse species (nineteen families) of small to medium sized (12–75 cm) shorebirds or waders are found around the world in a wide variety of marine, freshwater and terrestrial habitats. Many migrate long distances between feeding and breeding grounds. Although 116 species spend at least part of the year in Australia, only a small proportion are resident or breed here. Many are still in breeding plumage when they arrive — they soon don their less conspicuous non-breeding plumage. They congregate in large groups in wetlands and along the beaches, tidal mudflats and reefs of Australia's coastline, feeding on a variety of animals and plant materials. Many moult and gain breeding plumage before they depart. Some young birds remain in Australia for one to two years before joining migrating flocks. The few species that breed or are resident in Australia disperse and defend territories during breeding season.

The largest group (family: Scolopacidae, 48 species in Australia) are the long-legged waders with long bills — the snipes, godwits, curlews, shanks, sandpipers and their relatives. They breed in the Northern Hemisphere, in temperate to arctic latitudes and spend summer in Australia. They feed by probing their bills, of various lengths, into the mudflats and extracting shallow burrowers such as crabs, medium-burrowing shellfish, or deep-burrowing worms.

Of the nineteen species of plovers, dotterels and lapwings (family: Charadriidae) in Australia, the best known is the Masked Lapwing (*Vanellus miles*), because it aggressively defends its nest and chicks.

**Top:** Comb-crested Jacana (*Irediparra gallinacea*) spreads its weight across its long toes when trotting on lily pads. **Right:** The Masked Lapwing (*Vanellus miles*) is very protective of its nest and young.

**Clockwise from top left:** The Bush Stone-curlew (*Burhinus grallarius*) or "thick-knee" is renowned for its eerie nocturnal calls; A Common Sandpiper (*Actitis hypoleucos*) takes a little time out to survey its surroundings; Black-winged Stilt (*Himantopus himantopus*) breeds opportunistically when it rains inland; The Ruddy Turnstone (*Arenaria interpres*) is an animated feeder. It forages for invertebrates by flipping over stones and seaweed; The Pied Oystercatcher (*Haematopus longirostris*) uses its long bill to probe for invertebrates along beaches and estuaries around Australia.

# Gulls & Terns

### Order: Charadriiformes

The wader group also includes gulls and terns (family: Laridae, 95 species). Thirty-six are seen around Australian coastlines; a few also penetrate inland. Generally black, grey or white, they have long pointed wings and webbed feet. The largest are the skuas (53–65 cm) and jaegers (41–55 cm): aggressive predators that often harass smaller seabirds into regurgitating their food. They also prey on fish, squid, seabird eggs and chicks, and carrion. Seven species breed in Arctic or Antarctic waters. Two skuas and three jaegers range to southern Australian waters.

Far more abundant are the gregarious gulls and terns (about 86 species worldwide), which breed in enormous noisy colonies on offshore islands or inland lakes. Gulls are larger (27–66 cm) with broader wings and longer stronger legs than terns (21–55 cm). Opportunistic hunters of fish, crustaceans, offal and human food scraps, they also harass other seabirds into dropping their prey, and frequently scavenge around parklands and rubbish tips. Three gulls breed in Australia — the large endemic Pacific Gull (*Larus pacificus*), the Kelp Gull (*Larus dominicanus*) and the well-known Silver Gull (*Larus novaehollandiae*). Five others visit Australian waters.

Terns are slender with forked tails and long pointed wings. Coastal species plunge-dive for fish or snatch them from the water's surface; inland species feed on small land-dwelling vertebrates. Fourteen species breed in Australia, the most widespread being the Caspian Tern (*Sterna caspia*), Gull-billed Tern (*Sterna nilotica*), Crested Tern (*Sterna bergii*) and Common Tern (*Sterna hirundo*). Three more visit Australian waters.

**Top:** The Crested Tern (*Sterna bergii*), commonly seen around the Australian coastline. **Right:** A Common Noddy (*Anous stolidus*) incubating an egg on its nest — a scrape lined with sticks, coral and seaweed.

**Clockwise from top left:** The Pacific Gull (*Larus pacificus*) is the largest of Australia's gulls. It lives around southern shores; The Roseate Tern (*Sterna dougallii*) has a red-black bill, red legs and long white tail streamers; The adaptable Silver Gull (*Larus novaehollandiae*) has made its home around beaches, coastal parks and dumps and along inland waterways; Caspian Tern (*Sterna caspia*).

Australia also has two ternlets and five endemic noddies. Noddies differ from terns in their colouration: they are all grey or mostly grey. They rest on water and seize fish, sea jellies and plankton from the surface. Large colonies breed on coral cays, particularly along the Great Barrier Reef.

Pratincoles (family: Glareolidae, sixteen species) are short-legged waders of floodplains, deltas and pastures. Closely related to terns, they also fly fast and gracefully. They are unusual amongst waders in that they feed their young by regurgitating food onto the ground. Two visit Australia.

# Pigeons & Doves
## Order: Columbiformes

Pigeons and doves are plump birds with small heads and dense plumage; they usually have short necks and legs. A diverse group, over 300 species live around the world, 25 of them throughout Australia's varied habitats (including two introduced pigeon species). Although they vary widely in size and plumage, most feed on seeds, fruit, or both, supplemented with the occasional invertebrate.

The brightly coloured fruit-pigeons and fruit-doves of north-eastern Australia's closed forests range from the larger (35–50 cm) Wompoo Fruit-Dove (*Ptilinopus magnificus*) to the smaller (20–25 cm) Rose-crowned Fruit-Dove (*Ptilinopus regina*). These species process fruits without destroying the seeds and are important rainforest seed dispersers. Their guts are shorter than other pigeons' and doves', which have strong muscular gizzards for grinding food, assisted by swallowed grit. Other fruit-eaters including the Emerald Dove (*Chalcophaps indica*) and Topknot Pigeon (*Lopholaimus antarcticus*) grind and digest fruit flesh and seeds and play no part in seed dispersal.

The ground-feeding seed-eaters include forest, woodland and heath-dwellers, such as the Peaceful Dove (*Geopelia striata)* and Common Bronzewing (*Phaps chalcoptera*), and inhabitants of Australia's drier inland plains and grasslands including the Spinifex Pigeon (*Geophaps plumifera*) and Crested Pigeon (*Ocyphaps lophotes*). Pigeons are unusual amongst birds, in that they are able to drink water continuously, without raising their heads to swallow. This allows arid species to drink quickly at inland waterholes.

Strong fliers, many are nomadic and some are very gregarious, flocking in hundreds or thousands. Highly vocal, many repeat their cooing calls. Males are larger and more conspicuous than females. Male courtship displays include bowing and cooing and

**Top:** Peaceful Dove (*Geopelia stiata*).
**Left:** Wompoo Fruit-Dove (*Ptilinopus magnificus*).

**Clockwise from top left:** The Common Bronzewing (*Phaps chalcoptera*); The Crested Pigeon (*Ocyphaps lophotes*) lives across Australia; The Emerald Dove (*Chalcophaps indica*); The Rose-crowned Fruit-Dove (*Ptilinopus regina*) lives in the north and east. **Below:** Spinifex Pigeon (*Geophaps plumifera*), sometimes called the Plumed Pigeon due to its prominent head wear.

sometimes flying above females and producing clapping sounds with the wings. Parental care is prolonged and both sexes produce crop milk, which is rich in fats and proteins for their young — one or two initially helpless chicks that develop quickly but still need feeding.

Some of Australia's pigeons and doves are threatened by habitat destruction and feral predators — others have adapted well to urban development and inhabit parks and gardens.

# Cockatoos & Parrots

Order: Psittaciformes

Colourful plumage, high intelligence and sociability give cockatoos and parrots a special appeal. The more than 330 mainly tropical species (Australia has 56, including 44 endemics) are believed to be descended from Gondwanan ancestors. Two forward and two backward pointing toes allow these birds to climb trees and grasp food in their claws, manipulating it in their strongly hooked beaks. Nearly all species feed on seeds, fruits, nuts, flowers and nectar, in the trees or on the ground. Many form long-term pair bonds and congregate in large noisy feeding flocks, particularly outside breeding season.

## Cockatoos, Corellas & Cockatiel    Family: Cacatuidae

Cockatoos are large (34–64 cm long) and sturdy with short tails, heavy beaks and conspicuous crests, which they raise in alarm or excitement. They use their powerful bills to open hard seed capsules, dig up seeds buried in the ground or strip and tear bark and wood, allowing access to wood-boring insect larvae. Their skulls are distinctively different from other parrots. In most species, both sexes look alike. The world's eighteen species of cockatoos are found only in the Australasian region; fourteen live in Australia.

Of Australia's six black cockatoos, two have extremely prominent crests; the others are distinguished by differences in colouration particularly around their faces, breasts and tails. Seven other cockatoos are pink and grey, pink and white, or mostly white. The largest (44–51 cm) and best known is the mostly white Sulphur-crested Cockatoo (*Cacatua galerita*). The smallest (30–33 cm long) is the Cockatiel (*Nymphicus hollandicus*).

Cockatoos nest in tree hollows. While incubating, female black cockatoos are fed by the males. Amongst the other species, both sexes share incubation duties. Because of their habit of stripping trees and crops, some have historically been unpopular with (and illegally shot by) Australian farmers, despite their popularity with city folk. Others, particularly the Galah (*Cacatua roseicapilla*), have benefited from the extension of grasslands resulting from forest clearing and construction of dams in arid areas.

**Above:** The Yellow-tailed Black-Cockatoo (*Calyptorhynchus funereus*) lives across the south-east. **Right:** The Galah (*Cacatua roseicapilla*) ranges across the entire continent and half of Tasmania.

**Clockwise from top:** The Little Corella (*Cacatua sanguinea*) forms noisy feeding flocks; Sulphur-crested Cockatoo (*Cacatua galerita*); A Red-tailed Black-Cockatoo (*Calyptorhynchus banksii*) female displaying feathers; The Cockatiel (*Nymphicus hollandicus*) occupies most of the continent's drier regions.

Six species of lorikeets live amongst Australia's forests, woodlands, scrublands, heaths, mangroves and parks and gardens. These are the nectar-eating parrots. They have brush-tipped tongues and simplified intestinal systems perfect for collecting and digesting nectar and pollen. These highly energetic and nomadic birds often move long distances daily (up to 50 km) and seasonally as they follow the flowering of eucalypts, paperbarks, banksias, grevilleas and other native plants. They are often conspicuous feeders, foraging in noisy flocks and routinely swinging upside down to reach blossoms.

The best known are the Rainbow Lorikeet (*Trichoglossus haematodus*) and the slightly smaller and less colourful Scaly-breasted Lorikeet (*Trichoglossus chlorolepidotus*), which often move around together. Like the other smaller lorikeets, the Scaly-breasted Lorikeet is predominantly green but has red underwings. The more delicately coloured Varied Lorikeet (*Psitteuteles versicolor*) has slightly less delicate manners — flocks are known to greedily chase honeyeaters and other usurpers away from a tree in full bloom. Of the other three species, the Little Lorikeet (*Glossopsitta pusilla*) is the fastest flier, producing a whirring sound with its rapid wingbeats. The stockier Purple-crowned Lorikeet (*Glossopsitta porphyrocephala*) also creates this whirring sound. It can be distinguished in-flight by its red and blue underwings. The Musk Lorikeet (*Glossopsitta concinna*) is the largest of the three. It has a brilliant scarlet patch over its ear and forehead.

At 13–16 cm, the Double-eyed Fig-Parrot (*Cyclopsitta diophthalma*) is the smallest Australian parrot. Mostly green with a red forehead and eye patch, the males closely resemble the Little Lorikeet but are distinguished by the extent of the red face markings and the presence of blue in their plumage. Three subspecies of the fig-parrot live in isolated patches of rainforest, woodland and scrub along the east coast. Particularly partial to fig seeds, the fig-parrot extracts them from the fruits using its large bill. A quiet feeder, this species is amongst the lesser-known parrots.

**Top:** The northern subspecies of the Double-eyed Fig-Parrot (*Cyclopsitta diophthalma*). **Right:** A Scaly-breasted Lorikeet (*Trichoglossus chlorolepidotus*) feeding on a *Grevillea* species.

**DIET & HABITAT:** Like other lorikeets it is nomadic, following the seasonal flowering especially of eucalypts and banksias, in heaths, mangroves, woodlands and open and closed forests near the coast. It is a common visitor to cities and towns when eucalypts, banksias, paperbarks and other garden plants are flowering and fruiting. As well as pollen, nectar and fruit, it eats seeds and insects and their larvae.

**BEHAVIOUR & BREEDING:** Noisy flocks feed from sunrise, shelter during the heat of the day and roost together, often in the same trees at night. Pairs bond for life. During breeding season (August–January in the south and east, variable in the north) each pair nests in a tree hollow near water, scraping wood dust onto the bottom of the hollow. The female incubates the eggs (for 23 days), the male keeping her company. Both sexes feed the chicks, which fledge at about eight weeks.

**PREDATORS & THREATS:** These birds are agile but may fall prey to predatory birds such as the Brown Falcon and the Peregrine Falcon, and cats and foxes.

*All of the colours of the rainbow combine in the plumage of this appropriately named lorikeet, the first Australian parrot to be illustrated in colour — in Peter Brown's* New Illustrations of Zoology *published in 1774. The subspecies commonly encountered in eastern and south-eastern Australia (*T. h. moluccanus*) gives way to a second subspecies (*T. h. rubritorquis, the Red-collared Lorikeet) across the Top End. Other related colour forms live in New Guinea and on the South Pacific islands. The colour of the nape in particular varies with locality.*

**FEATURES:** The wholly brilliant blue head and lower belly are unique to this lorikeet species and make it easy to identify. The bird has an emerald-green back, red and orange breast and yellow underwing band.

**Top and above:** The Rainbow Lorikeet is one of Australia's best-loved birds, often seen and heard in gardens.

**LENGTH:** 25–32 cm
**NEST:** Tree hollow
**EGGS:** 2, white

**CALL:** Screeches, chatters
**MIGRATION:** Sedentary-nomadic
**STATUS:** Secure

# Eclectus Parrot  *Eclectus roratus*

*With red females and green males this large parrot long ago confused naturalists, who at one time believed the two sexes to be two separate species.*

**DIET & HABITAT:** The Eclectus Parrot lives in the canopy of rainforest and woodland in a small part of Cape York Peninsula and into New Guinea and the Solomons. It feeds on berries, other fruits, flowers, seeds and nuts.

**BEHAVIOUR & BREEDING:** Small flocks feed together and join large noisy roosts. Brooding pairs are assisted by other adults.

**LENGTH:** 40–43 cm
**NEST:** Tree hollow
**EGGS:** 2, white
**CALL:** Raucous screeche
**MIGRATION:** Sedentary
**STATUS:** Secure

# Australian King-Parrot  *Alisterus scapularis*

*This parrot is striking with its bright red, green and blue plumage. The male has a red head whereas the female's is green.*

**DIET & HABITAT:** This inhabitant of coastal and mountain forests feeds in the canopy mainly on seeds, particularly eucalypt and acacia seeds, fruit and flowers. It occasionally feeds on fallen seeds on the ground.

**BEHAVIOUR & BREEDING:** It is an elegant but wary bird. It flies swiftly with deep wingbeats. The female incubates the eggs for around twenty days.

**LENGTH:** 41–44 cm
**NEST:** Tree hollow
**EGGS:** 3–5, white
**CALL:** Pipes, screeches
**MIGRATION:** Sedentary-dispersive
**STATUS:** Secure

# Pale-headed Rosella  *Platycercus adscitus*

*Australia has a rosella representative for each State and Territory. The Pale-headed Rosella, with two subspecies (P. a. palliceps and P. a. adscitus) enjoys one of the largest distributions.*

**DIET & HABITAT:** Rosellas live in forests and woodlands around Australia. They feed on seeds, fruits, flowers, nectar and insects, frequently found on the ground.

**BEHAVIOUR & BREEDING:** These shy birds fly swiftly with a bouncy motion. Young remain with parents for many months.

**LENGTH:** 28–30 cm
**NEST:** Tree hollow
**EGGS:** 3–5, white
**CALL:** Pipes, screeches
**MIGRATION:** Sedentary
**STATUS:** Secure

# Australian Ringneck *Barnardius zonarius*

*This parrot, named for its yellow collar, has four subspecies — the Port Lincoln Parrot, the Twenty-eight Parrot, the Mallee Ringneck and the Cloncurry Ringneck.*

**DIET & HABITAT:** It inhabits eucalypt forests, woodlands, mallee and acacia scrubs, feeding on the ground or in the foliage on a variety of plant materials.

**BEHAVIOUR & BREEDING:** The subspecies interbreed where they overlap producing intermediate forms.

**LENGTH:** 34–37 cm
**NEST:** Tree hollow
**EGGS:** 4–7, white
**CALL:** Ringing
**MIGRATION:** Sedentary-nomadic
**STATUS:** Secure

# Orange-bellied Parrot *Neophema chrysogaster*

*One of the world's rarest birds, this parrot is sadly on the brink of extinction. It breeds in the isolated south-west Tasmanian wilderness then migrates to southern Australia. Both habitats are increasingly threatened.*

**DIET & HABITAT:** Surviving mainly in coastal habitats, this parrot's diet consists mostly of seeds.

**BEHAVIOUR & BREEDING:** Less than 200 birds including 50 permanent breeding pairs remain in the wild. Pairs share parental duties.

**LENGTH:** 20–22 cm
**NEST:** Tree hollow
**EGGS:** 4–6, white
**CALL:** Tinkles, buzzes
**MIGRATION:** Migratory
**STATUS:** Critically Endangered

# Budgerigar *Melopsittacus undulates*

*The "Budgie" is the best known of all parrots. This inland parrot congregates around waterholes to drink in the late afternoon. In the centre of Australia extremely large flocks occur.*

**DIET & HABITAT:** This nomadic bird inhabits grasslands, and scrublands of the arid interior. It feeds almost entirely on grass seeds.

**BEHAVIOUR & BREEDING:** The Budgie moves and breeds irregularly in response to rainfall — and rapid grass growth. In good seasons populations explode.

**LENGTH:** 17–20 cm
**NEST:** Hollow limb
**EGGS:** 4–6, white
**CALL:** Chirrups, chatters
**MIGRATION:** Highly nomadic
**STATUS:** Secure

# Cuckoos & Coucals

## Order: Cuculiformes

Of the world's species of cuckoos, two visit Australia as non-breeding migrants. Another eleven breed in the south then migrate inland or to northern Australia, New Guinea or beyond for winter. "Brood parasites", they lay their eggs in other birds' nests and often remove one or more of the host parents' eggs. Host parents incubate and brood the cuckoo young as their own. Cuckoos parasitise over 100 Australian bird species. Varying greatly in size (14–66 cm), most eat insects. Fast and graceful in-flight, they have distinctive calls.

## Channel-billed Cuckoo  *Scythrops novaehollandiae*

*Despite being different in size, diet and appearance to other cuckoos, this bird is a consummate brood parasite, one of only two species in Australia that lays more than one egg (sometimes up to five) in the same host nest. The other is the Common Koel,* Eudynamys scolopacea.

**FEATURES:** The size and shape of the Channel-billed Cuckoo's body and large down-curved bill are reminiscent of the hornbills of South-East Asia. However, it does have the characteristic cuckoo plumage patterns — mottled or dark above with barred undersides. Like other cuckoos it has a long tail and long droopy wings.

**DIET & HABITAT:** Unusually, this cuckoo is a fruit-eater, preferring figs and other native fruits, although it has been seen eating Magpie-lark (*Grallina cyanoleuca*) eggs and nestlings. It arrives in northern Australia in spring and moves southwards through eastern forests and woodlands. It prefers tall forests with fig trees. It returns to Indonesia or New Guinea in March–April.

**BEHAVIOUR & BREEDING:** Its raucous call, a rising "kawk" is often heard at night. Breeding season occurs from August to December. The largest of all parasitic birds, Channel-billed Cuckoos require large hosts such as currawongs, ravens, crows, and Magpie-larks. Laying females often smash host eggs. Young Channel-billed Cuckoos do not evict their nest-mates as other cuckoos do. Instead they develop quickly, demanding all of the food and out-competing any host chicks that eventually starve and die.

**PREDATORS & THREATS:** This cuckoo sometimes flies into windows. It is potentially limited by forest destruction, but may benefit from host population increases.

**Inset and above:** The Channel-billed Cuckoo is sometimes referred to as the Rainbird or Stormbird.

**LENGTH:** 58–66 cm
**NEST:** Hosts' nest
**EGGS:** 3–4, white-brown

**CALL:** Raucous "kawk"
**MIGRATION:** Summer breeding migrant
**STATUS:** Secure

# Pheasant Coucal
*Centropus phasianinus*

*Only the Pheasant Coucal has made its home in Australia; other species live mostly in the tropics of Africa and South-East Asia. Coucals were formerly assigned their own family in the order Cuculiformes but are now considered a subfamily of the Cuculidae family of cuckoos.*

**FEATURES:** This long-tailed but short-legged bird resembles the pheasants, hence its name. Outside breeding season its brown plumage is mottled and streaked. Both males and females take on the generally darker plumage with black head and breast in breeding season.

**DIET & HABITAT:** This is a grassland bird also found around the edges of swamps, in heath or dense low vegetation in gardens and on roadsides. It feeds on insects as well as a range of small vertebrates including frogs, lizards, mammals and young birds and eggs. It also lives in New Guinea.

**BEHAVIOUR & BREEDING:** The Pheasant Coucal calls with a deep descending "coop-coop-coop-coop-coop-coop-coop". Not a strong flier, it climbs to the top of a small tree and from there glides to the next. It builds its nest close to the ground but must fly and climb into nearby trees to gather materials. The resultant nest is a rough vegetation bowl

with a canopy concealed amongst grasses and 1–2 m off the ground. This arduous task is often undertaken twice in a breeding season (October–April). A second clutch is incubated in a second nest while the first clutch is fed nearby. Fledging in 13–14 days, the first brood is banished soon after.

**PREDATORS & THREATS:** Living mainly on the ground it often darts onto the road when alarmed and is hit by passing cars. Temporary loss of its limited flight abilities due to saturation from dew or rain can render it vulnerable to predators such as feral animals. Its low nest is easily raided by feral animals and other predators.

**Top:** Pheasant Coucal in breeding plumage.
**Left:** The dishevelled non-breeding plumage of the Pheasant Coucal.

**LENGTH:** 60–80 cm
**NEST:** Rough bowl
**EGGS:** 3–4, white

**CALL:** Repeated "coop"
**MIGRATION:** Sedentary
**STATUS:** Secure

# Owls

## Order: Strigiformes

Rounded heads with binocular vision, acute hearing and sharp beaks, feathered legs with strong talons and large wings with soft plumage that allow silent flight are the identifying characteristics of owls. These formidable nocturnal hunters are found in most habitats around the world. They feed on a variety of smaller vertebrates and invertebrates, captured either while patrolling their territories or by swooping upon them from perches. Some even catch fish at night. They generally kill their prey with their talons then swallow it whole, later regurgitating pellets containing indigestible materials. Owls commandeer disused nests of other birds or nest in tree hollows, caves or old buildings. Pairs usually form permanent pair bonds. Courtship may involve display flights, hooting duets or sharing tid-bits of food. Australia's ten species belong to two groups, the hawk-owls (family: Strigidae, five of 135 species) and the masked owls (family: Tytonidae, five of twelve species).

One of the most widespread of all land birds, living on every continent except Antarctica, is the Barn Owl (*Tyto alba*). This familiar owl, recognised by its pale heart-shaped face and dark eyes, is a consummate nocturnal hunter, capable of pinpointing prey in total darkness. Living in Australia's open habitats, it swoops silently on unsuspecting mice, rats and other small mammals, as well as insects, frogs, lizards and birds. It breeds infrequently, raising two to three clutches during periodic mouse plagues, but not breeding when mice are scarce.

**Top:** The Southern Boobook (*Ninox novaeseelandiae*).
**Right:** The Barking Owl (*Ninox connivens*).

## Powerful Owl    *Ninox strenua*

*Australia's largest owl, about the size of a small eagle, roosts during the day on large branches. Its rounded face is typical of the hawk-owls.*

**DIET & HABITAT:** The endemic Powerful Owl hunts in eucalypt forests, woodlands, and parks and gardens, taking kookaburras, and mammals such as flying-foxes, possums, and even cats. It tears it prey apart and eats it in smaller pieces.

**BEHAVIOUR & BREEDING:** Permanent pairs occupy and defend a large territory.

**LENGTH:** 60–66 cm
**NEST:** High hollow
**EGGS:** 2, white
**CALL:** Mournful "woo-hoo"
**MIGRATION:** Sedentary
**STATUS:** Secure

# Barking Owl  *Ninox connivens*

Named for its common night call, "wook-wook", in breeding season, the Barking Owl sometimes issues a blood-curdling scream.

**DIET & HABITAT:** This owl inhabits open forests, woodlands and scrubs extending inland. It hunts large insects, and tears apart large birds and mammals.

**BEHAVIOUR & BREEDING:** Pairs occupy permanent territories. The least nocturnal of Australian owls, it sometimes calls before sunset.

**LENGTH:** 35–45 cm
**NEST:** Hollow, rabbit burrow
**EGGS:** 2–3, white
**CALL:** "wook-wook"
**MIGRATION:** Sedentary
**STATUS:** Secure

# Southern Boobook  *Ninox novaeseelandiae*

Also known as the "Mopoke", due to its two-part call, this owl is Australia's smallest and most abundant.

**DIET & HABITAT:** Four subspecies exist and inhabit open forests, woodlands and scrub. They hunt invertebrates, particularly beetles and moths, and small birds and mammals.

**BEHAVIOUR & BREEDING:** Often heard but rarely seen, the Southern Boobook's call is a familiar night-time sound. Pairs roosting in trees or caves are sometimes mobbed by smaller birds during the day.

**LENGTH:** 25–36 cm
**NEST:** Tree hollow
**EGGS:** 2–3, white round
**CALL:** "mo-poke" or "boo-book'
**MIGRATION:** Sedentary
**STATUS:** Secure

# Grass Owl  *Tyto capensis*

Australia's five masked owls are less common than the hawk-owls. The rarest, the Grass Owl, also lives in New Guinea.

**DIET & HABITAT:** From dusk it flies low over coastal grasslands, heaths, swamps, wetlands and sugarcane fields, patrolling for rodents, marsupials and birds.

**BEHAVIOUR & BREEDING:** During the day, it roosts on the ground amongst grass tussocks. Nesting chambers are connected via runways or tunnels. Pairs breed more often during rodent plagues.

**LENGTH:** 33–38 cm
**NEST:** Mattress or tunnel of grass
**EGGS:** 4–5, white
**CALL:** Loud "cush-cush-sh-sh"
**MIGRATION:** Dispersive
**STATUS:** Secure

# Frogmouths & Nightjars
## Order: Caprimulgiformes

Frogmouths and nightjars are long-winged and long-tailed nocturnal birds. Like owls, they have soft feathers and fly silently, swooping on unsuspecting prey in the air or on the ground. However, as their feet are smaller and weaker and cannot grasp prey, they often scoop them up in their wide mouths. Hunting at dawn and dusk, they rest motionless in trees or on the ground during the day. Their mottled plumage provides exceptional camouflage. Australia is home to seven of about 110 species — three frogmouths (family: Podargidae) and four nightjars (families: Caprimulgidae and Aegothelidae).

## Spotted Nightjar   *Eurostopodus argus*

*Nightjars' loud calls are considered to "jar" the night, hence their common name. The Spotted Nightjar is the species most commonly seen along country roads at night. It has large buff spots on the ends of its wings, visible as it flies through headlight beams. Its eye-shine is pink-red.*

**FEATURES:** The most colourful of all nightjars, this bird's fluffy plumage is patterned with cream, rufous and black. Its camouflage is so complete that it often fools predators as it roosts on or near the ground amongst the leaf litter during the day.

**DIET & HABITAT:** The Spotted Nightjar is particularly common in inland mallee, Mulga and pine scrubs, and Spinifex country. It also lives in drier open forests and woodlands west of the Great Dividing Range — leaving the eastern coastal areas to the White-throated Nightjar (*Eurostopodus mystacalis*). It is most active just after dusk and before dawn, chasing moths, beetles and other insects. It may migrate within Australia and to New Guinea in winter.

**BEHAVIOUR & BREEDING:** Like other nightjars it is a swift flier, its long wings allowing it to turn and glide quickly in pursuit of prey. Pairs nest amongst leaf litter under trees, or on more open rocky ground, sharing parental duties.

**PREDATORS & THREATS:** This species relies on camouflage for self-defence, but in defence of chicks or a nest, a parent may spread its wings, fan its tail, puff out its throat and hiss.

**Top and above:** This species' camouflage colours are broken by its conspicuous white throat.

**LENGTH:** 29–33 cm
**NEST:** Scrape
**EGGS:** 1, yellow-green

**CALL:** Caws, gobbles
**MIGRATION:** Possible migrant
**STATUS:** Secure

# Tawny Frogmouth   *Podargus strigoides*

**DIET & HABITAT:** The Tawny Frogmouth lives in most forest, woodland and scrub habitats, except rainforest, throughout Australia. It also lives in New Guinea. It hunts insects, small frogs and lizards, relying on its keen eyesight and hearing to detect them. The margins of its feathers are softened to muffle the sound of its flight.

**BEHAVIOUR & BREEDING:** This bird lives alone, in pairs or in small family groups (5–6). Like the other Australian frogmouths, the Marbled (*Podargus ocellatus*) and Papuan Frogmouths (*Podargus papuensis*), it mates for life and lives in the same small territory throughout the year. Pairs build flimsy stick nests in tree forks in forest or parkland and sometimes along roadsides. Both parents incubate the eggs and feed the downy chicks. After breeding season, family groups may roost together on the same branch, their "oom-oom" call often the only clue to their presence.

**PREDATORS & THREATS:** If threatened while roosting, the Tawny Frogmouth usually fluffs out its feathers, opens its orange eyes, gapes its wide mouth and hisses at the intruder. Its habit of hunting around roadsides makes it a frequent component of roadkill.

*With its head tilted back and eyes closed to slits, the Tawny Frogmouth roosts motionless on stumps and branches during the day, resembling a broken branch. At night it hunts from a perch, watching intently for prey on the ground before gliding down to seize it.*

**FEATURES:** The eyes are orange and there are long bristles around the broad hooked bill, which is pale green inside. This frogmouth varies in size and plumage — the inland and northern subspecies (*P. s. plalaenoides*) is smaller with plainer grey than the mottled grey east coast subspecies (*P. s. strigoides*).

**Top:** Unlike owls, frogmouths have eyes that are situated on either side of its head. **Above:** The Tawny Frogmouth is a master of camouflage.

**LENGTH:** 33–50 cm
**NEST:** Stick nest
**EGGS:** 2–4, white

**CALL:** Resonant pulsing
**MIGRATION:** Sedentary
**STATUS:** Secure

# Kingfishers, Bee-eaters & Rollers
## Order: Coraciiformes

Full of character and presence, kingfishers are an essential part of the Australian bush. These large headed and large bodied birds have sturdy pointed beaks, short legs with partially fused toes and mostly long tails. Australia has at least ten of the world's species.

Technically only two are "river kingfishers" (family: Alcedinidae) — the regal Azure Kingfisher (*Alcedo azurea*) and the Little Kingfisher (*Alcedo pusilla*), the smallest (11.5–13 cm) of the group. These birds call as they patrol their feeding territories along rivers, creeks and mangroves. Using a number of favourite perches, they watch the water, waiting patiently for prey to appear, before plunge-diving dramatically and grasping the fish, crustacean or insect, in their long bills. Back on their perches they strike prey repeatedly before swallowing it head first. Indigestible parts are regurgitated as pellets.

The other species, including the kookaburras, are "forest kingfishers" (family: Halcyonidae). These birds hunt over land by sighting prey from a perch, dropping to seize it, and stunning it before swallowing it whole. The largest and best known is the Laughing Kookaburra (*Dacelo novaeguineae*). Of the smaller species, the Sacred Kingfisher (*Todiramphus sanctus*) and Forest Kingfisher (*Todiramphus macleayii*) are the best known. The Buff-breasted Paradise-Kingfisher (*Tanysiptera sylvia*) is a summer breeding migrant from New Guinea.

Bee-eaters (family: Meropidae, 24 species) and rollers (family: Coraciidae, eleven species) share kingfishers' basic design features. Australia has one species of each. The Rainbow Bee-eater (*Merops ornatus*), often seen in small groups resting on fences, usually eats several hundred bees and other stinging insects each day. The robust Dollarbird (*Eurystomus orientalis*), named after the large pale coin-shaped patch under each wing, is a summer breeding migrant from New Guinea and eats moths, cicadas and beetles.

**Top:** The Azure Kingfisher (*Alcedo azurea*) is a consummate fisher. **Right:** The Rainbow Bee-eater (*Merops ornatus*) specialises in capturing stinging insects.

*The loud call of the Laughing Kookaburra is this country's most famous birdcall and one of the defining sounds of the Australian bush. Males of neighbouring groups call at dawn and dusk to advertise their territories, often vying with each other in alternate branches of the same tree, or flying past each other in dispute.*

**FEATURES:** This is the largest of the world's 90 kingfishers and one of the most vocal. Its plumage is predominantly brown and white but with small patches of blue over its brown wings. The closely related Blue-winged Kookaburra (*Dacelo leachii*) has far more blue on its wings and a blue rump; males also have a blue tail. It lacks the brown eye patch.

**DIET & HABITAT:** The Laughing Kookaburra lives in woodland, open forest, around timbered creeks and in parks and gardens in eastern and southern Australia. The Blue-winged Kookaburra lives in similar habitat across the northern half of coastal Australia. Both prey on insects and other invertebrates, lizards, snakes, small birds and mammals.

**BEHAVIOUR & BREEDING:** This sedentary bird lives in family groups comprised of a breeding pair and their offspring. Older offspring assist by defending territorial boundaries, incubating eggs and feeding and caring for younger siblings. They remain in this auxiliary role for up to four years before establishing territories for themselves and producing their own offspring. Adults may live up to twenty years. Both species nest in tree hollows or arboreal termite mounds (August–January).

**PREDATORS & THREATS:** Kookaburras' social system means that they do not produce as many offspring as they otherwise might. Habitat destruction or the use of pesticides may therefore cause marked declines in their numbers. Nest predators include pythons and goannas.

**Top:** The Laughing Kookaburra, an Australian icon. **Above:** The more frantic laughing call of the Blue-winged Kookaburra is less melodic than the famous call of the Laughing Kookaburra.

**LENGTH:** 41–47 cm
**NEST:** Hollow, arboreal termite mound
**EGGS:** 3, white

**CALL:** Raucous laughter
**MIGRATION:** Sedentary; Blue-winged — Sedentary
**STATUS:** Secure

# Swifts & Swiftlets

## Order: Apodiformes

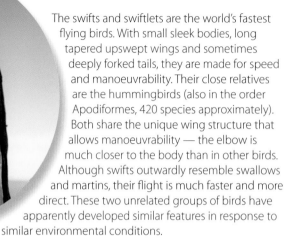

The swifts and swiftlets are the world's fastest flying birds. With small sleek bodies, long tapered upswept wings and sometimes deeply forked tails, they are made for speed and manoeuvrability. Their close relatives are the hummingbirds (also in the order Apodiformes, 420 species approximately). Both share the unique wing structure that allows manoeuvrability — the elbow is much closer to the body than in other birds. Although swifts outwardly resemble swallows and martins, their flight is much faster and more direct. These two unrelated groups of birds have apparently developed similar features in response to similar environmental conditions.

Spending most of their lives on the wing, swifts are also the world's most aerial birds. A few species remain airborne for months, sleeping while gliding in circles, but most land to roost or nest. Unlike the swallows and martins, which are passerines, swifts cannot perch. Instead they cling to cliffs, cave walls, tree trunks or foliage at night, gripping tightly with their strong curved claws. Some species have all four toes pointing forwards to help them cling to vertical surfaces; in others the hindtoe is reversible. Many prop themselves on their short spine-tipped tails to increase stability.

Swifts hunt on the wing by scooping small insect prey — mosquitoes and gnats — into their wide beaks. Most hunt at dawn and dusk but cave-dwelling swiftlets may continue through the night, using echolocative clicks emitted from their mouths to navigate. Large feeding flocks fly exceptionally high, sometimes rising to several thousand metres to capture prey that has risen on thermals. Many species are migratory. Most nest in colonies, building tiny nests of cobwebs, moss and saliva onto cave walls, tree hollows or chimneys. Eggs are partially incubated.

Three species regularly occur in Australia — one resident, the White-rumped Swiftlet (*Collocalia spodiopygius*), and two summer migrants, the Fork-tailed Swift (*Apus pacificus*) and White-throated Needletail (*Hirundapus caudacutus*). Three others occur irregularly.

**Top:** Fork-tailed Swift.

# Perching Birds
## Order: Passeriformes

More than half of all bird species belong to the order Passeriformes, also called perching birds. The diversity of birds in this group is extensive. Size alone can vary enormously with some species weighing a few grams while others weigh in excess of a kilogram. Songbirds are notable members of this order. They possess well-developed vocal organs although not all songbirds are considered as melodious as their name suggests.

**Above:** Gouldian Finch.

# Swallows & Martins   Family: Hirundinidae

Swallows and the smaller martins are elegant birds usually seen darting and manoeuvring over water in pursuit of insects. With long tapered wings and sometimes deeply forked tails, they resemble the unrelated swifts and swiftlets (the non-passerine order Apodiformes). Although they spend much time in the air, their flight is slower and they feed much closer to the ground. More efficient hunters than swifts, they pursue large insects — flies, beetles, butterflies — aerially and capture them individually in their wide beaks. They usually drink by flying over pools and scooping water in their beaks, and bathe by skimming and dipping into the water.

As with passerines, swallows' and martins' toe arrangements allows them to perch. These gregarious birds are often seen settled in rows on overhead wires, television aerials or dead branches. Many feed and roost in groups, keeping in touch with chirruping contact calls. Courting males issue high-pitched twitters from perches. Most of the world's 80 species are migratory, following insect prey, some travelling over 10,000 km from Europe to South Africa or from Canada to Brazil in cooler months, returning to breed when the weather warms.

Australia has four residents. The best known is the Welcome Swallow (*Hirundo neoxena*) found throughout much of the country, but particularly common in the south. It builds its cup-shaped mud nest under eaves, on cave walls or in cliff cavities. The White-backed Swallow (*Cheramoeca leucosternus*), Australia's only endemic, lives inland and tunnels into earth banks to roost and nest. The Tree Martin (*Hirundo nigricans*) lives in forested areas and feeds above the canopy in small noisy groups. It nests in tree hollows and migrates northwards for winter. The Fairy Martin (*Hirundo ariel*) is a grassland inhabitant; it builds long bottle-shaped mud nests under eaves, bridges and cliff overhangs.

**Right:** Tree Martins form small colonies, nesting in hollows of large old trees like River Red Gums.

# Lyrebirds   Family: Menuridae

Lyrebirds appear to have no close avian relatives elsewhere in the world and are thought to have evolved on this continent. Behaviourally, they are amongst the most majestic and interesting bird species. Australia has two lyrebird species. Albert's Lyrebird (*Menura alberti*) lives only in a small area of forest in NSW and Qld. The Superb Lyrebird (*M. novaehollandiae*) ranges from Victoria along the east coast to Southern Qld.

**Top:** The Superb Lyrebird has a long, ornate tail.

# Superb Lyrebird   *Menura novaehollandiae*

*This elusive bird is a true songster. Males are renowned for their striking displays — with their lacy tails fanned over their heads in a lyre shape, they turn circles, shimmering their tails and calling for females in a medley of mimicry and song. A range of loud and clear bird and mammal sounds are incorporated with the unique repeated phrases, and sometimes mechanical noises as well. Females can also sing and mimic, though less impressively than the males .*

**FEATURES:** The Superb Lyrebird has grey plumage whereas the slightly smaller Albert's Lyrebird (*Menura alberti*) is more chestnut-coloured. Males of both species develop their long tails (up to 60 cm and 50 cm respectively) at 6–8 years. Females also have long tails but without the distinctive lacy display plumes.

**DIET & HABITAT:** Both species have restricted distributions in south-eastern Australia. They inhabit temperate to subtropical wet eucalypt forests particularly around damp, dark ferny gullies at altitudes of up to 1500 m. They forage for invertebrates by scratching amongst leaf litter and excavating rotting logs.

**BEHAVIOUR & BREEDING:** Males display to females from midwinter (June–August) atop their mounds of scratched earth 1.5 m high and almost 1 m wide (Superb Lyrebird) or platforms of trampled vines (Albert's Lyrebird). Mating takes place nearby but males play no part in nest building, incubation (six weeks) or the brooding (six weeks) of the single chick. The nest is a complex dome of sticks, ferns and moss built on the ground, in a tree fern, or on a rock or tree stump. Males mate with more than one female. In spring, males moult their tails. In summer, lyrebirds form loose feeding groups. Young, which accompany their mothers, apparently learn the songs of their elders.

**PREDATORS & THREATS:** Predation by cats, dogs and foxes, habitat clearing and weed invasion have led to marked declines.

**LENGTH:** 86–100 cm

**NEST:** Stick dome with moss roof

**EGGS:** 1, grey-brown-purple

**CALL:** Mellow, far-carrying medley

**MIGRATION:** Sedentary

**STATUS:** Secure

# Pittas, Scrub-birds & Treecreepers
## Families: Pittidae, Atrichornithidae & Climacteridae

These three families of passerines are small elusive birds of the forest floor and undergrowth, usually in dense moist forests such as rainforests or mangroves. They all feed on leaf litter invertebrates; pittas also eat fruit and berries and treecreepers also eat seeds. Their feeding behaviours and songs are distinctive.

The brightly plumed pittas characteristically hop along the ground, tossing leaves aside. Renowned for their habit of striking snails on rocks to make it easier to access the flesh, they litter the forest floor with broken shells. Roosting high in the canopy, they often call from there. Some species migrate seasonally between lowlands and highlands, or across the open sea, at night. Widespread across Australia and New Guinea, Asia and Africa, four of the world's 26 species live in Australia, and one — the Rainbow Pitta (*Pitta iris*) — is endemic. The best known is the Noisy Pitta (*Pitta versicolor*).

Scrub-birds live only in restricted parts of Australia, spending most of their time on the forest floor. The Noisy Scrub-bird (*Atrichornis clamosus*) flicks leaves over or flushes insects out of the leaf litter. The Rufous Scrub-bird (*Atrichornis rufescens*) pokes its head and sometimes its body under leaf litter while foraging. Possibly related to lyrebirds, males defend small territories with loud, penetrating songs incorporating mimicry. Females are usually silent.

Six of seven species of the vocal treecreepers live in Australia's diverse forests, woodlands and scrubs. With strong legs and feet, they "shuffle-run" up tree trunks and along the undersides of low branches in search of insects, particularly ants, probing cracks and crevices with their long curved beaks. Gliding from tree trunk to tree base, most also feed on the ground. Often seen in family groups, breeding is usually cooperative with two or three males feeding the chicks of one female.

**Top:** The elusive Noisy Pitta (*Pitta versicolor*) is more often heard than seen.
**Above, left to right:** Rufous Treecreeper (*Climacteris rufa*) in-flight; The loud ringing calls of the Brown Treecreeper (*C. picumnus*) are commonly heard.

# Fairy-wrens, Emu-wrens & Grasswrens   Family: Maluridae

Twenty-five species of small brightly plumed birds that hold their sparse tails erect are found throughout Australia and New Guinea. They are closely related to the pardalote family and the honeyeaters. Curious and agile, they are all insectivorous, feeding on mantids, dragonflies and other large insects. They are all communal, living in family groups where males and often older siblings assist by feeding chicks, making it possible for females to raise several clutches each season. Males are brightly plumed during breeding season, but take on dull eclipse plumage for the rest of the year. Nine fairy-wrens, three emu-wrens and ten grasswrens share Australia's diverse habitats.

The best known are the fairy-wrens, existing only in Australia and New Guinea; some of which have adapted well to human habitation, frequenting parks and gardens. Family groups are often seen hopping over the ground briskly or foraging amongst low vegetation in parks and gardens. Emu-wrens have unique tails comprised of six coarse plumes that, like Emu feathers, lack the hooks that normally hold the barbs of feathers together. Two species live amongst Spinifex in the arid inland, climbing the grass stems to keep lookout and scurrying away through grass clumps. The other lives amongst grass tussocks and low shrubs in coastal heaths. The larger grasswrens also live mostly amongst Spinifex and other low vegetation. Well camouflaged, with colour varying from almost black to grey, they all bear white streaks along their plumage.

**Top:** A male Superb Fairy-wren (*Malurus cyaneus*) in breeding plumage. This is one of Australia's best-loved birds.

## Superb Fairy-wren   *Malurus cyaneus*

*A bright blue cap, eye patch and mantle, black mask and deep blue neck, back and tail comprise males' breeding plumage. Females are brown with chestnut lores.*

DIET & HABITAT: Living in forests, woodlands, heaths and parks and gardens, each family group's territory usually contains shrubby undergrowth and open areas. A variety of insects is eaten.

BEHAVIOUR & BREEDING: Family groups may contain several adult males. Chicks leave the nest while tail-less.

LENGTH: 13–14 cm
NEST: Grass ball
EGGS: 3–4, white
CALL: Trills, other calls
MIGRATION: Sedentary
STATUS: Secure

# Splendid Fairy-wren *Malurus splendens*

During breeding season male Splendid Fairy-wrens are almost completely blue. For the rest of the year they are brown with blue tails and wings. Females have orange lores.

DIET & HABITAT: The Splendid Fairy-wren lives amongst the undergrowth in grasslands, dry scrublands and woodlands where it forages for a variety of insects.

BEHAVIOUR & BREEDING: Males maintain territory year round. More than one male tends the female's nest (September–January).

LENGTH: 12–14 cm
NEST: Grass ball
EGGS: 3–4, white
CALL: Trills, soft calls
MIGRATION: Sedentary-partly nomadic
STATUS: Secure

# Variegated Fairy-wren *Malurus lamberti*

Males in breeding plumage have a blue-purple crown and mantle and a chestnut shoulder patch. The plumage of the females is unique amongst fairy-wrens, varying from brownish-grey with chestnut lores to blue-grey with white lores.

DIET & HABITAT: Five subspecies live in a range of habitats, foraging for insects.

BEHAVIOUR & BREEDING: Usually seen in pairs or parties, this species breeds throughout the year after rain.

LENGTH: 11–14.5 cm
NEST: Grass ball
EGGS: 3–4, white
CALL: Trilling
MIGRATION: Mostly sedentary
STATUS: Secure

# Red-backed Fairy-wren *Malurus melanocephalus*

The smallest of the fairy-wrens is also the most striking. Males in breeding plumage are black with a scarlet to crimson back.

DIET & HABITAT: Inhabiting undergrowth in a variety of habitats including grasslands, woodlands, rainforest margins, mangroves and swamps, the two subspecies capture a variety of insects on the ground or in the shrubbery.

BEHAVIOUR & BREEDING: Several clutches may be raised in warmer months. After breeding, groups of 30–40 forage widely.

LENGTH: 10–13 cm
NEST: Grass ball
EGGS: 3–4, white
CALL: Soft reels
MIGRATION: Sedentary
STATUS: Secure

Despite the lack of external similarities, DNA analysis has determined that this assemblage of small birds, including pardalotes, scrubwrens, thornbills and gerygones, is closely related. Of 67 species, 47 occur in Australia, many of them endemic. This is the second largest family of birds in Australia (after the honeyeaters).

Pardalotes are tiny (8–12 cm) birds with short blunt bills, short tails and bold markings, particularly spots and striations. Spending most of their time in the canopy of forests, woodlands, scrubs, mangroves, parks and gardens, they are rarely seen. All four species are endemic to Australia. The Forty-spotted Pardalote (*Pardalotus quadragintus*), endemic to Tasmania, is endangered.

Gerygones are small (9–13 cm) insect-eating warblers. Eight species are found in Australia. They feed by hovering outside the foliage of trees in forests, woodlands, scrubs and mangroves. They sing distinctive sweet plaintive melodies in minor key. The genus name *Gerygone* is Greek for "born of sound".

Scrubwrens (11–15 cm) also forage for insects on the ground or amongst branches in restricted areas of rainforests, woodlands, heaths, mangroves and parks and gardens. Closely related are the heathwrens and fieldwrens of the drier woodlands and scrubs. These birds, capable of mimicry, sing with clear sweet voices.

Thornbills (9.5–13 cm) are active insect and seed-eating warblers of Australia's woodlands. Twelve species are found in Australia; one is also found in New Guinea. Similar to thornbills and often occurring in mixed flocks with them are three endemic boldly marked whitefaces. They sing with tinkling voices.

At 8–9 cm long, the Weebill (*Smicrornis brevirostris*) is Australia's smallest bird. It resembles the thornbills and the gerygones and may be an ancestral form of both. It lives in drier woodlands and scrubs.

The Rockwarbler (*Origma solitaria*) is the only bird restricted to New South Wales. The Pilotbird (*Pycnoptilus floccosos*) often accompanies the Superb Lyrebird.

The three bristlebirds (17–27 cm long) have stiff bristles near their bill bases. They are often confused with scrub-birds despite their rufous markings and frequently fanned tails. Their clear calls carry over a distance.

**Top:** The Western Gerygone (*Gerygone fusca*) forages in the tree canopy and can be found in open forests, woodlands, Mulga and mallee. **Right:** The Striated Pardalote (*Pardalotus striatus*) lives over much of Australia.

# Spotted Pardalote  *Pardalotus punctatus*

*A creek bank or road cutting dotted with small tunnels is a curious sight. Yet these are the earth-tunnel nests of the Spotted Pardalote. Some pairs return to the same nests year after year.*

**FEATURES:** This is the most colourful of the pardalotes. Jewel-like white spots adorn its dark upper body. Males' throats are yellow and rumps are red (subspecies *P. p. punctatus*) or yellow (subspecies *P. p. xanthopygus*). Females have pale underparts.

**DIET & HABITAT:** Like the three other species, the Forty-spotted Pardalote (*Pardalotus quadragintus*), Red-browed Pardalote (*Pardalotus rubricatus*) and Striated Pardalote (*Pardalotus striatus*), it spends most of the day in the canopies of eucalypt trees. It forages there for lerps or scale insects (small, leaf-sucking insects) and other small invertebrates including moths, caterpillars, beetles and spiders, amongst the foliage.

**BEHAVIOUR & BREEDING:** Generally living in pairs or family parties, outside breeding season this species migrates, following lerp outbreaks, moving in large mixed flocks (10–20, sometimes in the hundreds) with other pardalotes, particularly the Striated Pardalote, and thornbills. These flocks have been observed moving through the canopy slowly, flitting from one tree to the next. This tiny bird flies swiftly with fast shallow wingbeats.

Males choose the nest site and both sexes dig the tunnel 0.5–1.5 m long into a creek bank, steep slope or around the roots of a mallee tree. At the end they build a neat oval-shaped twig nest, where they rear their three or four young. The other pardalotes also nest in tunnels, tree hollows, animal burrows or disused nests of the Fairy Martin (*Hirundo ariel*).

**PREDATORS & THREATS:** Like other pardalotes, this small bird is frequently chased by larger honeyeaters because it competes for food and manna gum. It is often preyed upon by cats and has been known to fly into windows. Forest clearing and logging may reduce its range.

**LENGTH:** 8–10 cm
**NEST:** Tunnel
**EGGS:** 3–4, white

**CALL:** Piping
**MIGRATION:** Migratory-nomadic
**STATUS:** Secure

Restricted to the Australasian-Oceanic region, honeyeaters are believed to have originated in Gondwana. With 72 of 178 species, this is the largest passerine family in Australia. This versatile family plays an important role in the pollination and seed dispersal of native plants and the control of insect infestations.

Plumage is generally dull green to brown, often with patches of white or yellow on the face, neck or both. The most colourful is the diminutive Scarlet Honeyeater (*Myzomela sanguinolenta*, 10–11 cm). The largest are the wattlebirds (26–45 cm) and friarbirds (25–37 cm). All have long down curved bills adapted to deeply probing flowers, and long tubular tongues ending in brush-like fibres. As well as lapping nectar (up to ten laps per second), they use their tongues to reach into bark crevices for sap, manna and the sweet exudates of plant-sucking insects. Spinebills (12–16.5 cm) have particularly long bills.

Nectar-feeding species may be highly nomadic, following the flowering of their favoured trees, or may feed generally on species as they come into flower. Some honeyeaters eat mainly insects, berries and fruit, including mistletoe fruit. Six to twelve species with complementary feeding styles usually share the food resources in any given habitat.

Honeyeaters are active, aggressive and territorial, often chasing larger intruders away from food resources. Calls vary markedly, from simple single notes to complex songs, but they are all vocal. Generally forming long-term pair bonds, females or pairs incubate eggs (fourteen days) and raise chicks (fourteen days). Nestlings sometimes receive morsels from non-breeding adults.

Chats are small (10–13 cm) colourful birds included in the honeyeater family; most possess brush-tipped tongues. They walk or run and feed close to the ground on insects and seeds. The five species are all endemic to Australia. Four live inland in drier habitats; the Gibberbird or Gibber Chat (*Ashbyia lovensis*) lives on the open gibber plains right in the arid centre. Only one species is coastal, preferring wetter ground — the White-fronted Chat (*Epthianura albifrons*).

**Top:** The Red Wattlebird (*Anthochaera carunculata*) is commonly encountered in southern mainland Australia. **Right:** The Brown Honeyeater (*Lichmera indistincta*) is found in a diverse range of habitats, mainly feeding on nectar.

**Clockwise from top:** The White-plumed Honeyeater (*Lichenostomus penicillatus*) lives in coastal woodlands and dry creek beds through the interior; The Noisy Friarbird (*Philemon corniculatus*) is a noisy species, gregarious except in breeding season; The Eastern Spinebill (*Acanthorhynchus tenuirostris*) has a long fine bill ideal for feeding on grevillea nectar; Male Scarlet Honeyeaters (*Myzomela sanguinolenta*) are striking but females are plain brown.

# Bell Miner  *Manorina melanophrys*

*This small inconspicuous honeyeater is the elusive bellbird of south-eastern Australia. Its loud tinkling carries for long distances through the forest, allowing individuals to stay in contact with other flock members.*

**DIET & HABITAT:** This species lives in eucalypt forest and thick woodland with dense undergrowth, usually with water nearby. It feeds in the canopy predominantly on the sugary white coverings secreted by lerps. It also catches spiders and sips nectar.

**LENGTH:** 19 cm
**NEST:** Frail cup
**EGGS:** 2–3, pale pink
**CALL:** Loud tinkling
**MIGRATION:** Sedentary
**STATUS:** Secure

**BEHAVIOUR & BREEDING:** Dense colonies occupy the same territory for many years, actively excluding other species to protect the lerps. If the lerps damage the foliage excessively colonies move away for several years. Females build nests but several adults feed the chicks, even after they leave the nest. Young can fend for themselves from about 30 days.

# Lewin's Honeyeater  *Meliphaga lewinii*

*This rainforest honeyeater lives permanently at altitudes of over 200 m in north Queensland, but in Victoria it is an altitudinal migrant, moving from the highlands (over 1000 m) to the lowlands in autumn–winter. It has a large distinctive semicircular ear patch.*

**DIET & HABITAT:** Lewin's Honeyeater also lives in lowland forests, woodlands, scrubs (particularly brigalow), heaths, mangroves, canefields, orchards and parks and gardens. Native fruits are its main food, but it also eats insects and nectar in the canopy.

**LENGTH:** 19–21 cm
**NEST:** Deep cup
**EGGS:** 2–3, off-white
**CALL:** Rolling chatter
**MIGRATION:** Altitudinal migrant
**STATUS:** Secure

**BEHAVIOUR & BREEDING:** Individuals or small groups are highly aggressive towards each other and other honeyeater species. This bold species has been known to enter houses. Its loud "machine-gun" call is well known by bushwalkers. It usually breeds between August and January.

# Blue-faced Honeyeater   *Entomyzon cyanotis*

This large honeyeater usually commandeers the abandoned nests of the Grey-crowned Babbler (Pomatostomus temporalis), a bird given to building multiple nests. Conversely, the nest is then parasitised by the Channel-billed Cuckoo (Scythrops novaehollandiae).

**LENGTH:** 30–32 cm
**NEST:** Deserted nest
**EGGS:** 2–3, pink-buff
**CALL:** Whistle "kweep"
**MIGRATION:** Sedentary-local migrant
**STATUS:** Secure

**DIET & HABITAT:** The Blue-faced Honeyeater, named after the patch of bare blue skin around its eye, moves amongst eucalypt forests, woodlands, rainforest edges, paperbark swamps and mangroves, foraging for insects, nectar, pollen and fruit. It is also known as the Banana Bird. More common in northern than southern Australia, it also lives in New Guinea.

**PREDATORS & THREATS:** This honeyeater is usually seen in pairs, small groups or flocks of up to 30 with other honeyeaters. It is aggressive towards smaller birds and steals nesting materials from them. Only rarely does it build its own untidy bark bowl-shaped nest.

# Crimson Chat   *Epthianura tricolor*

The most widespread of the chats runs quickly over the ground in search of insects in Australia's arid shrublands. The male is conspicuous with his dark back, red crown, under parts and rump. The female is cinnamon and brown.

**LENGTH:** 10–12 cm
**NEST:** Neat cup
**EGGS:** 3, white-pink
**CALL:** Chimes, rattles
**MIGRATION:** Highly nomadic
**STATUS:** Secure

**DIET & HABITAT:** One of Australia's most nomadic birds, the Crimson Chat moves in response to rainfall. Mainly an inland species, it irregularly visits parks and gardens along the coast. Insects are captured on the ground or in low shrubs. It also feeds on the nectar of desert plants as it migrates across deserts largely devoid of insects.

**BEHAVIOUR & BREEDING:** The male's courtship display flight involves hovering over the female and swooping towards her with wings and tails spread wide and crown-feathers erect. Pairs share nest building and parental duties. After breeding (June–October, or after rain) family parties congregate in small flocks.

Australia is home to about 21 of 46 robin species confined to Australasia and Oceania. They are believed to have spread into this area 35 million years ago. Although they are named after European robins (family: Muscicapidae, the flycatchers), because of their similar appearance and behaviour, they are not closely related.

Small (11–18 cm), graceful and delicately plumed, the Australian robins brighten forests and gardens with simple pleasant songs. Generally the sexes are alike, but in some species males are more striking. All pounce on or catch insects and invertebrates on the wing. Like the flycatchers, their bills are triangular shaped and surrounded by bristles. Most stand upright as they perch, characteristically flicking or lowering their wingtips or tails.

Of the four yellow robins, the best known is the Eastern Yellow Robin (*Eopsaltria australis*), widespread through eastern Australia. Its genus name, *Eopsaltria*, means "dawn harpist"; this robin is usually the first to sing in the morning and the last to fall silent at night. Bold individuals often approach picnickers or forage for insects around gardeners.

Another widespread and popular species is the charming Jacky Winter (*Microeca fascinans*). It is often seen swooping after insects or hovering and pouncing on them, before returning to its perch and wagging its tail. It regularly sits on paddock fences and boldly feeds around humans and other animals.

The Scarlet Robin (*Petroica mulitcolor*) has the widest distribution of all the Australasian Robins. It often feeds amongst charred vegetation in recently burnt areas of eucalypt forest. Males sing boldly from conspicuous perches. Australia has four other red or pink-breasted robins.

The Australian contingent also includes three grey/black and white robins, a brown robin and two thrush-like scrub-robins that are more adapted to living on the ground. Most species are sedentary, but a few are dispersive or move seasonally. Most live only for two years.

**Top:** The Scarlet Robin (*Petroica multicolor*) is the best-known red robin. **Right:** An Eastern Yellow Robin (*Eopsaltria australis*) with a tasty morsel for its young offspring.

*This is the smallest and most vibrantly plumed of the Australian robins. Also one of the most active, it is characteristically restless and fluttery, making short flights and flicking its wings and tail while perching.*

**FEATURES:** Like the other red robins, the males have black backs and wings, red breasts and white underparts. However, this species' red cap gives the males a much more striking appearance. The females, typically nondescript grey-brown with paler underparts, have a smaller orange-brown cap.

**DIET & HABITAT:** Widely distributed over southern and central Australia, the Red-capped Robin inhabits drier scrubs and woodlands — particularly mallee, Mulga, cypress pine and sheoak communities — as well as eucalypt forests, parks and gardens. In winter it moves to wetter coastal areas. It hunts by perching on low branches and pouncing on all manner of insects on the ground. Alternatively, it stirs them up amongst the leaf litter by shuffling its foot or waving its wing, or it snaps up insects while on the wing.

**BEHAVIOUR & BREEDING:** A quiet but curious bird, it is usually seen singly, in pairs, or in mixed flocks with other small insectivores including thornbills, fantails and whistlers. Like most other Australian robins, females build the cup-shaped nests and are fed by males as they incubate (fourteen days, July–January). Both parents usually care for chicks (a further fourteen days). This species builds the smallest and neatest grass and bark nest, lined with fur and feathers and camouflaged with spiders' web and lichen. Nests often contain the eggs of Australia's smaller cuckoo species. Birds disperse after breeding, many moving between the inland and the coast.

**PREDATORS & THREATS:** Parents defend nests by flying into the faces of intruders and attempting to distract them, often feigning broken wings. At other times, adults are equally bold with territorial intruders, flitting in front of them.

**LENGTH:** 11–12 cm
**NEST:** Neat cup
**EGGS:** 2–3, blue-grey

**CALL:** Insect-like trilling
**MIGRATION:** Migratory
**STATUS:** Secure

The logrunner and whipbird families live mostly on the forest floor in family groups or small colonies. With short rounded wings, they are poor fliers, but their robust legs afford speed on the ground. Most (ten species) are endemic to Australia and New Guinea; one lives only in Australia.

The Australian Logrunner (*Orthonyx temminckii*) and Chowchilla (*Orthonyx spaldingii*) are the only members of the logrunner family. Both live in rainforests, the Australian Logrunner in south-eastern Australia (and New Guinea) while the Chowchilla is endemic to Tropical North Queensland. They are plump bodied with feather shafts extending beyond their tails as spines. They scratch vigorously amongst the litter layer for invertebrates — mainly beetles, crustaceans and snails — and sometimes prop themselves on their tails to scratch with both feet alternately. Both call loudly with distinctive calls; the Chowchilla is an excellent mimic.

Fairly closely related to them is the whipbird family, also very vocal with unmistakeable calls. The Eastern Whipbird's (*Psophodes olivaceus*) call is one of Australia's distinguishing bush sounds. Males and females of the Western Whipbird (*Psophodes nigrogularis*) sing sweetly in duet for several minutes, particularly during winter. Whipbirds are boldly patterned with crests and long tails. Mated pairs of the plainer and almost identical Chiming (*Psophodes occidentalis)* and Chirruping Wedgebills (*Psophodes cristatus*) also maintain vocal contact by singing in duet. The four boldly plumed quail-thrushes are very secretive; when threatened, birds freeze, run or fly with quail-like whirr to safety. Courting males sing from perches.

A third family, the Australian babblers (four species), also live in small noisy groups (3–12) on the forest floor or low in vegetation. They scour the soil searching for insect larvae or hop along trunks and low branches probing crevices in the bark for insects, spiders and other invertebrates. They also eat small frogs, reptiles and seeds. These gregarious birds nest cooperatively with many group members feeding the young. A fifth species closely resembling the whipbirds lives only in New Guinea.

**Right:** The rarely seen Logrunner (*Orthonyx temminckii*).

*This iconic species is more often heard than seen. Its most distinctive call is a mated pair's duet, the female usually answering the male's loud whip crack with two ringing notes. The male is one of the east coast forests' noisiest birds, also producing a range of whistling songs.*

**FEATURES:** Males and females have the same plumage — a black upper body, head and crest with a white patch on the throat sides, and olive-green wings, back and white-tipped fantail. Males are larger than females.

**DIET & HABITAT:** Two subspecies, one southern (*P. olivaceus olivaceus*) and one northern (*P. olivaceus lateralis*) live amongst dense undergrowth in eastern Australia's rainforests, wet eucalypt forests, scrubs and heaths, particularly along creeks and gullies. This whipbird spends most of its time hopping bouncily over the ground, turning over leaf litter with its feet or probing amongst fallen logs for various insects and their larvae. It sometimes forages amongst foliage or low on tree trunks.

**BEHAVIOUR & BREEDING:** This secretive but lively and inquisitive bird is sometimes seen briefly by bushwalkers. It moves along the ground with its tail cocked and partly fanned. Rarely flying, it raises its crest when alarmed and runs when disturbed. The Western Whipbird is much shier. Both are very territorial. Pairs call to maintain contact and advertise territory.

Breeding in August to December, the female builds the loosely woven twig nest 0.5–3 m above the ground. The male feeds her as she incubates the eggs (eighteen days). Both parents feed the black downy hatchlings (twelve days). The male Western Whipbird collaborates in all stages of parenting.

**PREDATORS & THREATS:** Ground predators include snakes, goannas, feral cats, foxes and pigs. Following extensive habitat clearing, burning and stock grazing, the Western Whipbird is now critically endangered. The Eastern Whipbird has been more fortunate; more of its habitat remains.

**LENGTH:** 25–31 cm
**NEST:** Shallow bowl
**EGGS:** 2, pale blue

**CALL:** Whip crack & 2 rings
**MIGRATION:** Sedentary
**STATUS:** Secure

# Whistlers, Shrike-thrushes & Sittellas
## Family: Pachycephalidae & Neosittidae

Most of the 47 species of the whistler family are concentrated in Australia and New Guinea, but a few live in South-East Asia and across the South Pacific. They are all high-spirited songsters, varying in style from the explosive whistlers to the mellow shrike-thrushes. The most unique call is the deep tolling of the male Crested Bellbird (*Oreoica gutturalis*), a ground-dweller of the arid inland and mallee scrubs. With a diet mainly of insects and other invertebrates, occasionally supplemented by fruits, the bills of these tree-dwelling birds are typically robust and surrounded by bristles to sense prey or funnel their food. Unlike other insectivores they eat leisurely, picking insects from the surface of leaves or bark or off the ground. Usually sedentary, a few species follow altitudinal or inland-coastal migrations.

The small (15–19 cm) boldly patterned endangered Crested Shrike-tit (*Falcunculus frontatus*) lives high in eucalypt trees and feeds by prising the bark and snatching exposed insect larvae with its strong bill. It sings with a clear piping voice.

Australia's eight whistlers live in forests, woodlands, scrubs, heath, mangroves, parks and gardens. They vary considerably in size (14–22 cm) and plumage. The most widespread is the Rufous Whistler (*Pachycephala rufiventris*). This highly vocal bird announces the arrival of spring with its joyous courting song, sung by both males and females as they bow and display.

Of Australia's four shrike-thrushes, the most widespread is the Grey Shrike-thrush (*Colluricincla harmonica*), named for its clear far-carrying, pure-toned and rhythmic melodies. This bird forages actively amongst the trees and on the ground for insects, small lizards and mammals and occasionally young birds.

The small sittellas are thought to be related to the whistlers, but are classified in their own family. Only one of the world's three species lives in Australia — the Varied Sittella (*Daphoenositta chrysoptera*, 11–12.5 cm). Small flocks (up to nine individuals) work their way down trunks and branches foraging for insects and spiders under the bark. Breeding cooperatively, several birds build the nest and feed the chicks.

**Top:** A Golden Whistler female tending its nest —
the female is much duller than its male counterpart.

*The Golden Whistler lives across southern and eastern Australia and its coastal islands, as well as from Indonesia through New Guinea to Fiji. Across this range it is highly variable in plumage, with more subspecies than any other bird. In Australia alone, six are recognised.*

**FEATURES:** This species is named for the male's golden underparts and nape. The male of the nominate subspecies (*P. p. pectoralis*) has a black head and breast band, white chin, olive-brown wings and back with a grey-black tail. The female is grey-brown above with paler underparts. However, other subspecies vary in colour or lack the breast band and collar and in some subspecies the females are similar to males.

**DIET & HABITAT:** The Golden Whistler is an adaptable bird. It lives and breeds in the mountain rainforests of eastern Australia through a range of forest and woodland types to the mallee and brigalow scrubs of southern and western Australia. It also inhabits mangroves, orchards, parks and gardens. It hops slowly from branch to branch whilst foraging for insects and their larvae, and occasional berries.

**BEHAVIOUR & BREEDING:** For most of the year, this species is solitary or occurs in mixed-species groups. In autumn–winter, populations follow north–south, coastal–inland or altitudinal migration routes. During breeding season (August–January) males and females display and sing vigorously to proclaim their breeding territories, sometimes joined by their young. Like the Rufous Whistler (*Pachycephala rufiventris*), this species often sings after peals of thunder or similarly loud noises. Males may breed before they acquire full adult plumage at three years of age. Nests are frail twig bowls loosely bound by spiders' web, well concealed in a fork or thick foliage of a shrub or small tree.

**PREDATORS & THREATS:** This attractive bird is very bold. Nevertheless logging, fire regime changes, habitat fragmentation, predation by cats and car collisions have led to a reduction of its range.

**LENGTH:** 16.5–18.5 cm
**NEST:** Frail bowl
**EGGS:** 2–3, creamy-white

**CALL:** Sweet notes
**MIGRATION:** Sedentary-migratory
**STATUS:** Secure

These birds have broad bills, often flattened and usually surrounded by numerous bristle feathers that guide prey into the bill. Insects, larvae and/or spiders are caught on the wing during acrobatic manoeuvres, picked off leaves and bark or snatched off the ground after hovering above them. All are lively songbirds.

Twelve species of monarch flycatchers live in or visit Australia's wetter forests, woodlands and mangroves. Varying in size and plumage all bear black face masks. The largest and most familiar is the Magpie-lark or Peewee (*Grallina cyanoleuca*), only recently recognised as a monarch, due to the fact it builds a mud-nest. It was for many years grouped with the Australian mud-nest builders in the family Corcoracidae. This widely distributed species is often seen puddling in shallow water. Both sexes have black and white plumage, males with white eyebrows and females with white foreheads and throats. Mating pairs lift their wings and spread their tails as they sing their territorial duets. The name "Peewee" originates from the sound of this species' call.

The Yellow-breasted Boatbill (*Machaerirhynchus flaviventer*), with its extremely broad flat bill, is found only in Far North Queensland and New Guinea. It is one of only two boatbills in the world. The Spangled Drongo (*Dicrurus bracteatus*) is the only one of 24 mostly tropical drongos found in Australia. It is a summer breeding migrant from New Guinea. This glossy black bird is an aerial acrobat, swooping and twisting after insect prey, or diving and calling in courtship display.

Fantails are active flycatchers with large tails. The biggest, most widespread and most familiar is the bold Willie Wagtail (*Rhipidura leucophrys*), which catches insects close to the ground and consumes large numbers of butterflies. Like the flycatchers, fantails are keen songsters.

**Top:** A Rufous Fantail (*Rhipidura rufifrons*) tends its nestlings.  **Right:** The Willie Wagtail's call sounds like "sweet pretty creature".

**Clockwise from top:** A Satin Flycatcher (*Myiagra cyanoleuca*) incubating; A Grey Fantail (*Rhipidura fuliginosa*) at its fibrous cup nest; The Spangled Drongo (*Dicrurus bracteatus*) has a distinctive "fish tail"; The Magpie-lark (*Grallina cyanoleuca*) is better known to many Australians as the Peewee.

# Cuckoo-shrikes  Family: Campephagidae

Confusingly named, since they are neither cuckoos nor shrikes, this Afro-Asian family of passerines is actually related to the orioles. Nevertheless, their bodies are shaped like cuckoos' and their short strong bills resemble shrikes'. The seven species living in Australia — four cuckoo-shrikes, the Cicadabird and two trillers — have predominantly grey, black and white plumage. Most are tree-dwellers feeding mainly on insects supplemented with fruit and seeds. They are cooperative breeders that sometimes commandeer the nests of other birds, particularly the Magpie-lark's mud-nest.

**Right:** The White-bellied Cuckoo-shrike (*Coracina papuensis*) is not a cuckoo or a shrike.

# Black-faced Cuckoo-shrike  *Coracina novaehollandiae*

*The most widespread and familiar of Australia's cuckoo-shrikes is the Black-faced Cuckoo-shrike. With long pointed wings, this bird has strong undulating flight. It can hover into the wind and dive like a kestrel to collect prey. Like other members of this group it shuffles its wings when it lands on branches, probably to realign its flight feathers.*

**FEATURES:** This species is identified by its black face and chin, with the amount of black varying from individual to individual. Both sexes look alike.

**DIET & HABITAT:** Found across Australia from the arid inland to coastal parks and gardens, it also lives in Indonesia, New Guinea and the Solomon Islands. It eats insects gleaned off foliage, caught on the wing or pounced on from above, as well as fruit and berries. Some smaller birds chase this species; it may also occasionally eat nestlings.

**BEHAVIOUR & BREEDING:** Cuckoo-shrikes are usually seen alone, in pairs or small groups. In autumn, large flocks migrate inland or to northern Australia, New Guinea or Indonesia for the winter. Part of the population remains in southern woodlands, occupying communal roosts. Breeding pairs (August–February) defend nests aggressively. Young may be fed by adults other than their parents.

**PREDATORS & THREATS:** Before building a nest a pair usually spends a lot of time testing prospective forks in the chosen tree. Because nests are tiny, nestlings often get blown to the ground during heavy winds.

**LENGTH:** 30–36 cm
**NEST:** Tiny saucer
**EGGS:** 2–3, blue-green-olive

**CALL:** Musical rolling
**MIGRATION:** Sedentary-migratory
**STATUS:** Secure

# Orioles & Figbird    Family: Oriolidae

The Oriole family comprises 25 species of graceful forest canopy-dwellers mostly found across Afro-Asia and Australia. These red-eyed fruit and insect eaters have (often red) down-curved bills and long pointed wings allowing swift undulating flights above the canopy. They are seldom seen but being proficient singers, their clear fluty or bubbly songs travel through the forest. Australia's three members are more subtly plumed than overseas species. The orioles are more solitary, moving in pairs or trios, whereas the endemic Figbird is more gregarious.

**Right:** Female Figbirds lack the bright plumage of the males.

## Olive-backed Oriole    *Oriolus sagittatus*

*This excellent mimic is distinguished from the Yellow Oriole (Oriolus flavocinctus) by its white under parts.*

**DIET & HABITAT:** The Olive-backed Oriole inhabits forests, woodlands, parks and gardens, ranging inland to mallee scrubs, and to New Guinea. It eats small fruits and insects.

**BEHAVIOUR & BREEDING:** Following fruiting cycles, the eastern subspecies (*O. s. sagittatus*), migrates northwards and inland to breed in winter; northern subspecies (*O. s. affinis* and *O. s. magnirostris*) are more sedentary.

**LENGTH:** 26–28 cm
**NEST:** Deep cup
**EGGS:** 2–3, cream-brown
**CALL:** Soft "orry-orry-ole", mimicry
**MIGRATION:** Sedentary-migratory
**STATUS:** Secure

## Figbird    *Sphecotheres viridis*

*Males display a yellow throat and breast (S. v. flaviventris) or a grey throat, white belly and green flanks (S. v. vieilloti).*

**DIET & HABITAT:** The tropical "yellow" Figbird and eastern "green" Figbird feed around the edges of forests, woodlands, mangroves and in parks, gardens and orchards on native figs and cherries and cultivated fruits.

**BEHAVIOUR & BREEDING:** Sexes share parental duties (September–February). Flocks of 20–50 young birds chase each other noisily through the trees or feed together.

**LENGTH:** 27–30 cm
**NEST:** Twig-vine hammock
**EGGS:** 2–3, green-grey
**CALL:** "tu-tu heer"
**MIGRATION:** Locally nomadic
**STATUS:** Secure

Black-tipped blue-grey bills and black, grey and white plumage are the only obvious external features shared between woodswallows and the much larger butcherbirds, magpies and currawongs. However, these songbirds possess very similar skull structures and are closely related.

These gregarious birds live alone, in pairs or small family groups and nest, sometimes communally, in cup-shaped twig nests. Twenty species are distributed from Australia through Melanesia to India; fourteen occur in Australia, nine of them endemic.

Woodswallows are typically 12–20 cm long. Their plumage is grey and brown with black and white markings. They have long pointed wings and are the only songbirds that spend long periods of time soaring. Feeding mainly on insects caught on the wing, they nevertheless possess brush-tipped tongues for feeding on nectar and pollen. They are also unique amongst the songbirds in lacking preen glands. Instead, special feathers on their bellies grow continuously, breaking down into a fine water-resistant powder, known as powder down. When woodswallows preen themselves, they distribute this powder through their feathers.

These gregarious birds may be seen in small groups or flocks numbering in the thousands, sometimes with other woodswallow species. They are generally vocal, chattering to maintain contact, and are able to mimic other birds. Woodswallows typically roost communally and nest in loose colonies (August–January). Males and females of most species fan and rotate their white-tipped tails in courtship display, and share parental duties. Unrelated birds may assist with the brooding of chicks.

The Australian Magpie, butcherbirds (four species) and currawongs (three species, all endemic) are amongst Australia's finest songbirds. Their warbling, yodelling and carolling melodies are virtually synonymous with the Australian bush. Opportunistic but less carnivorous than the crow family, they often scavenge around picnic areas. The Australian Magpie and butcherbirds often nest communally in summer in parks and gardens; many Australians have encountered their aggressive dive-bombing defence. In contrast, currawongs are shy around their nests, preferring to defend their young by deception. Their antics and songs are also very familiar to most Australians.

**Top:** The White-breasted Woodswallow (*Artamus leucorynchus*) is often seen aerially feeding in small flocks or perched side by side on powerlines.  **Right:** Grey Butcherbirds (*Cracticus torquatus*) have a white marking between the eye and beak.

# Pied Butcherbird  *Cracticus nigrogularis*

*The Pied and Grey Butcherbirds (C. torquatus) are endemic, while the Black and Black-backed Butcherbirds (C. quoyi, C. mentalis) are also found in New Guinea.*

**DIET & HABITAT:** The Pied Butcherbird lives in woodland and dry scrub. It pounces on insects, small mammals, birds and reptiles.

**BEHAVIOUR & BREEDING:** Butcherbirds live alone, in pairs or small family groups. Males and females often sing duets. Nests are defended vigorously by dive-bombing. Juveniles are brown and cream.

**LENGTH:** 32–36 cm
**NEST:** Untidy bowl
**EGGS:** 3–4, white
**CALL:** Flute-like whistle
**MIGRATION:** Sedentary
**STATUS:** Secure

# Australian Magpie  *Gymnorthina tibicen*

*Australia's five subspecies have differing amounts of white on their backs.*

**DIET & HABITAT:** Found anywhere with trees and open ground, the Magpie probes the soil and turns up sticks or stones in search of insects, particularly scarab beetles. It also eats seeds and carrion.

**BEHAVIOUR & BREEDING:** Small groups (2–24 individuals) defend territories (2–18 hectares). Often only one female successfully raises offspring sired by the dominant male. Individuals breed at 4–5 years.

**LENGTH:** 38–44 cm
**NEST:** Bowl
**EGGS:** 3–4, pale blue-green-grey-brown
**CALL:** Carols, mimics
**MIGRATION:** Sedentary-locally nomadic
**STATUS:** Secure

# Pied Currawong  *Strepera graculina*

*The Pied Currawong is mostly black with white windows in its wings and undertail and a white tipped tail.*

**DIET & HABITAT:** Currawongs typically breed in high country forests and woodlands (August–December). Many disperse in large noisy flocks (over 100 individuals) to the lowlands. They eat almost anything, including fruit, insects, eggs, nestlings and human food scraps.

**BEHAVIOUR & BREEDING:** Nesting in pairs, parents care for fledglings for several months.

**LENGTH:** 42–50 cm
**NEST:** Bowl in eucalypt
**EGGS:** 3, brown-pink
**CALL:** "curra-wong", calls in-flight
**MIGRATION:** Migratory-dispersive
**STATUS:** Secure

# Bowerbirds & Birds of Paradise
## Family: Ptilonorhynchidae & Paradisaeidae

Bowerbirds are unique in their habit of building courtship bowers, and the birds of paradise are distinctive for their extravagant plumage and complex courtship displays. These two unrelated families are endemic to Australia, New Guinea and the Moluccas; Australia is home to ten of nineteen bowerbirds and four of 43 birds of paradise.

A diverse group, Australia's bowerbirds vary in size from the Green Catbird (*Ailuroedus crassirostris*, 24–32 cm) to the Great Bowerbird (*Chlamydera nuchalis*, 34–38 cm). Plumage varies markedly. Living in a variety of forests and woodlands, their diets include flowers, fruits, leaves, nectar and occasionally insects. Calls vary from cat-like yowls to rasping and rattling sounds and medleys of song and mimicry.

Males spend breeding season constructing intricate bowers and performing elaborate courtship rituals. Females build nests and raise chicks alone. Males generally breed serially. Bowers vary greatly, from a simple "stage", a small cleared patch decorated with fresh pale leaves (Tooth-billed Bowerbird, *Scenopoeetes dentirostris*) to the elaborate three metre tall "maypole bower" of the Golden Bowerbird (*Prionodura newtoniana*) constructed around two small trees. Most build "avenue bowers" — two parallel arched walls of sticks and grass stems, decorated with flowers, feathers, berries, shells, leaves or plastic items. The Green (*Ailuroedus crassirostris*) and the Spotted Catbird (*A. melanotis*) are interesting exceptions — monogamous pairs share parental duties and no bower is built, although in the past they probably built stage bowers.

Likewise, male birds of paradise display and mate, but offer no assistance with parenting. Australia's contingent have glossy black-green or black-purple plumage. All forest-dwellers, two are endemic to Australia — the Paradise Riflebird (*Ptiloris paradiseus*) and Victoria's Riflebird (*Ptiloris victoriae*). Male riflebirds typically stand erect on a perch with their wings curved and sway or open and shut their wings while calling loudly. Paradise Riflebirds produce a loud "crack" as they clap their wings together; when females approach they are encircled in the males' wings. Mating follows. In contrast, the Trumpet Manucode (*Manucodia keraudrenii*) breeds monogamously.

**Top:** The male Satin Bowerbird (*Ptilonorhynchus violaceus*) typically decorates its avenue bower with blue objects.
**Right:** The female Satin Bowerbird has cryptic plumage.

**Clockwise from top:** The call of the Green Catbird (*Ailuroedus crassirostris*), a southern species, resembles a wailing cat; The Magnificent Riflebird (*Ptiloris magnificus*) is found on Cape York Peninsula; The strikingly plumed male Regent Bowerbird (*Sericulus chrysocephalus*) has one of the least elaborate bowers; The Spotted Catbird (*Ailuroedus melanotis*) is endemic to Far North Queensland.

Members of the large crow family (family: Corvidae, 117 species) — jays, jackdaws, ravens and crows — live in Europe, Asia, Africa and North America. Highly intelligent birds, they are very adaptable and very sociable. Australia has five native species; all except the Torresian Crow are endemic.

Australia's representatives are commonly known as crows, although scientifically speaking, three are ravens. All five have glossy black plumage and white eyes. The ravens are larger than the crows and have longer throat hackle feathers. Crows have white down at the base of their neck feathers, whereas ravens possess grey-brown down; this is visible when the birds preen. The calls of the five species are subtly different.

The Forest Raven (*Corvus tasmanicus*) is the largest of the group (52–54 cm), with the largest bill and the shortest tail. It lives in forest patches in south-east Australia. The Little Crow (*Corvus bennetti*) is the smallest (48–50 cm); an inland nomad it occasionally migrates to the coast. The Little Raven (*Corvus mellori*) is another nomad that inhabits cooler areas in the south-east. The sedentary and more widespread Australian Raven (*Corvus coronoides*) has the largest throat hackles; they form a shaggy bunch under its chin as it calls. The similar Torresian Crow (*Corvus orru*) lives a sedentary life around coastal and inland waters in northern Australia and New Guinea.

Between them, Australia's ravens and crows occupy most habitats including cities. Opportunistic omnivores, they devour everything from fruit and grain to carrion, to small invertebrates and vertebrates. These birds are monogamous with permanent pair bonds. Breeding occurs in spring or after suitable rains in large stick nests built in tall trees or on windmill platforms or the like. Males feed incubating females (three weeks). Both parents brood the 4–5 chicks for 4–6 weeks.

**Top:** Torresian Crow.  **Below, left to right:** Little Crow; Australian Raven.

# Australian Mud-Nest Builders   Family: Corcoracidae

Closely related to the crow family are the Australian mud-nest builders — the endemic Apostlebird (*Struthidea cinerea*) and White-winged Chough (*Corcorax melanorhamphos*). Both species live in forests, woodlands and scrubs in noisy close-knit family groups. The White-winged Chough prefers mallee country, whereas the Apostlebird has a preference for native pine, myall and brigalow communities. Groups spend a lot of time on the ground, foraging for seeds and invertebrates such as snails, insects, spiders, millipedes, and dust bathing regularly. Communal breeders, they cooperate to build large bowl-shaped mud-nests, reinforced with grasses. All group members, including juvenile members up to four years old, incubate and brood the combined clutches. Up to three clutches are raised each breeding season. Large groups of both species congregate in winter, and the two species associate together where their ranges overlap.

**Right:** The Apostlebird (*Struthidea cinerea*) was originally thought to live in groups of twelve.

# Larks, Pipits & Wagtails   Family: Alaudidae & Motacillidae

Larks (90 species) are drab seed and invertebrate eaters of grasslands and plains. Although distributed widely around the world, only one occurs naturally in Australasia — the Singing Bushlark (*Mirafra javanica*). Males sing powerfully while perched on fences or stumps or hover over grasslands delivering a stream of mimicry and song. The Common Skylark (*Alauda arvensis*) is an introduced species.

Closely related, pipits (43 species) and wagtails (twelve species) are also widely distributed. Both vigorously hunt insects. Pipits run along the ground and stop to bob and wag their tails; wagtails wag their long tails up and down as they run with their heads bobbing. Courting males of Australia's single resident pipit, the Australian Pipit (*Anthus novaeseelandiae*), trill as they flutter above their territories then dive to the ground. Another pipit, the Red-throated Pipit (*Anthus cervinus*) occasionally visits from Asia. Two species of wagtail visit Australia in summer — the Yellow Wagtail (*Motacilla flava*) and Grey Wagtail (*Motacilla cinerea*).

**Left:** Singing Bushlark (*Mirafra javanica*).

Recent research has determined that sparrows and grassfinches are closely related. Australia has two introduced sparrows — the House Sparrow (*Passer domesticus*) and the Eurasian Tree Sparrow (*Passer montanus*). Eighteen native grassfinches and mannikins occupy Australia's grasslands, heaths, scrubs, woodlands, mangroves, farms, parks and gardens near water. These are small (10–14 cm) birds with short conical bills adapted to cracking open hard grass seeds and grasping small insects. Highly gregarious, particularly outside breeding season, they feed in small to large flocks and congregate at water holes to drink. Many are local or seasonal nomads. With their bold plumage, flocks are eye-catching particularly when they rise into the air in alarm. Forming strong pair bonds, many mate for life. Parents share incubation and brood duties. Most nest in loose colonies, making small ball-shaped grass nests but the Gouldian Finch (*Erythrura gouldiae*) nests in tree hollows or termite mounds.

The most widespread is the Zebra Finch (*Taeniopygia guttata*). It prefers drier areas including gibber plains, Spinifex grasslands and Mulga and saltbush scrubs in the arid interior. The Painted Finch (*Emblema pictum*) is another inland species. The remainder live closer to the coast. The Double-barred Finch (*Taeniopygia bichenovii*) has an owl-like face with distinctive white cheeks bordered with black. The reddest in colouring is the Crimson Finch (*Neochmia phaeton*). The Diamond Firetail (*Stagonopleura guttata*) has white diamond-shaped markings on its sides. The Gouldian Finch, the most colourful, has several colour forms with black, red or golden heads. Of the three native mannikins, the best known is the distinctively plumed Chestnut-breasted Mannikin (*Lonchura castaneothorax*).

The Nutmeg Mannikin (*Lonchura punctulata*), an aviary escapee, competes with native species for food and habitat; several including the Zebra Finch have suffered declines. Although native, the Chestnut-breasted Mannikin has become feral in some places. Sadly, the Gouldian Finch has suffered severe declines following habitat destruction, feral animal predation and a recent mite infestation, and is now endangered.

**Top:** A male Crimson Finch (*Neochmia phaeton*). The female is predominantly olive-brown with red highlights.
**Right:** A male Star Finch (*Neochmia ruficauda*).

**Clockwise from top left:** The
Chestnut-breasted Mannikin (*Lonchura
castaneothorax*) lives in wetter coastal
areas; A male Zebra Finch (*Taeniopygia
guttata*), this species lives across most
of Australia; Double-barred Finches
(*Taeniopygia bichenovii*) are active feeders,
they drink hourly; A male Diamond Firetail
(*Stagonopleura guttata*), the female has
brown eye-rings.

# Sunbirds
Family: Nectariniidae

Sunbirds (118 species) live across the tropics and subtropics between Africa and South-East Asia. These small colourful nectar-eating birds have slender down-curved bills, with which they pierce or probe flowers. They also consume vast quantities of spiders plucked from their webs. Australia has only one representative, which also lives between the Solomon Islands and China.

**Right:** Female Yellow-bellied Sunbird.

# Yellow-bellied Sunbird
*Nectarinia jugularis*

*This very conspicuous acrobatic bird is a favourite resident of tropical Queensland. Fearless and inquisitive, it nests around houses, even entering them in search of spiders and insects. It resembles the hummingbirds (order: Apodiformes) but flies with slower wingbeats.*

**FEATURES:** The female Yellow-bellied Sunbird has olive upper body parts and bright yellow underparts. The male is similar but has a shiny blue-black throat and breast.

Both have long curved bills housing tubular brush-tipped tongues perfect for lapping nectar.

**DIET & HABITAT:** This species lives around the edges of rainforest and in mangroves, paperbark woodlands and other thick coastal vegetation as well as in parks and gardens. The sunbird sucks the nectar of flowers, and it also preys on insects.

**BEHAVIOUR & BREEDING:** The Yellow-bellied Sunbird is usually seen singly or in pairs darting around its natural and garden habitats with swift direct flight, issuing its distinctive "tzit-tzit-tzit" call. The female builds a pendulous nest, incubates the eggs and feeds the chicks. The male is very encouraging but offers little practical assistance until the chicks are a week old. Pairs raise two to three clutches each season.

**PREDATORS & THREATS:** Hatchlings often fall prey to the Black Butcherbird (*Cracticus quoyi*), which visits repeatedly, forcing breeding pairs to relocate. Cats, rats and pythons are its other predators. This species benefits from the establishment of parks and gardens.

**LENGTH:** 11–12 cm
**NEST:** Long untidy "spindle'"
**EGGS:** 2–3, green-grey

**CALL:** Kiss-squeaks
**MIGRATION:** Sedentary
**STATUS:** Secure

# Mistletoebirds    Family: Dicaeidae

Otherwise known as flowerpeckers, 58 species in this family live through South-East Asia and New Guinea. The single Australian species is the Mistletoebird (*Dicaeum hirundinaceum*), which feeds primarily on mistletoe fruits. The pied male has a striking red throat and breast. The female is grey above and white below.

This tiny nomadic bird follows the fruiting of mistletoes, supplementing its diet with insects, nectar, pollen and other fruits. This bird lacks a gizzard, thus mistletoe seeds are quickly deposited on branches, and later germinate. Australia's 60 species of mistletoes depend on it to disperse their seeds.

Females build the suspended pear-shaped nest and incubate eggs. Chicks are fed on insects. Threats include shooting, habitat destruction, the control of mistletoe in parks and gardens as well as cats, foxes and larger birds.

**Right:** The Mistletoebird also eats berries, pollen and insects.

# White-eyes    Family: Zosteropidae

Eighty-two very similar species of white-eyes are dispersed through Africa, Asia and the Pacific islands. The most widespread of Australia's three species is the Silvereye. There are five Silvereye subspecies (*Zosterops lateralis lateralis, Z. l. chlorocephala, Z. l. ramsayi, Z. l. familiaris, Z. l. gouldi*) each of which show subtle plumage variations.

Silvereyes live amongst bushes and shrubs in parks, gardens and orchards. They feed low in the shrubbery on fruits, seeds, nectar (using brush-tipped tongues) and insects, including aphids and grubs.

Some subspecies are partly nomadic or migratory, migrating in large flocks at night. Winter flocks disperse in spring to breed. Pairs defend territories with determined warbling songs.

Predators include the Laughing Kookaburra (*Dacelo novaeguineae*). This species' penchant for orchard fruit and habit of spreading weed seeds have made it unpopular but it may be an important native plant disperser and predator of insect pests.

**Left:** The Silvereye (*Z. l. chlorocephala*) has the conspicuous eye-rings typical of white-eyes.

About 400 species of songbirds from Europe, Africa, Asia and Australia, including the Nightingale, are grouped together. Although many are small, brown and nondescript, all have strong rich voices. Ten old world warblers spend at least part of the year in Australia. These small to medium sized birds with pointy tails live mostly in grasslands and swamps. They feed on insects, small invertebrates, seeds and other plant material. Males display conspicuously during breeding season, singing heartily and often performing spectacular display flights over their territories. One of the most vocal is the Clamorous Reed-Warbler (*Acrocephalus stentoreus*), a summer breeding migrant. It calls incessantly with a rich fluid voice. The male Tawny Grassbird (*Megalurus timoriensis*) displays spectacularly — it shoots straight up into the sky singing continuously, hovers briefly then plunges back into cover. Likewise male cisticolas conduct fluttery song-flights. The songlarks sing from fence posts or in the air and the endemic Spinifexbird (*Eremiornis carteri*) sings atop Spinifex clumps.

Found across much of the world, thrushes (300 species) are medium sized songbirds with serene or melodious voices. They flick leaf litter or stomp heavily, then listen and plunge their bills into the soil in pursuit of worms or grubs. Australia has two natives, the Bassian Thrush (*Zoothera lunulata*), which ranges to Siberia and the South Pacific, and the endemic Russet-tailed Thrush (*Zoothera heinei*). Both are rainforest birds. The Common Blackbird (*Turdus merula*) and Song Thrush (*Turdus philomelos*) were introduced.

Starlings and mynas (106 species) are glossy medium sized usually insectivorous ground-feeding songbirds that occur from Polynesia to Africa. Their voices are wheezy or rattling but many whistle or mimic. They are gregarious species, foraging in flocks and nesting in colonies. The Metallic Starling (*Aplonis metallica*), a summer breeding migrant, is Australia's only native. It feeds on fruit, seeds, insects and nectar throughout tropical Queensland's rainforests. Most but not all of the birds return to New Guinea in autumn; some overwinter in Australia.

**Top:** A Metallic Starling (*Aplonis metallica*) at its nest.
**Right:** Brown Songlark (*Cincloramphus cruralis*) males display from high vantage points.

**Clockwise from top:** An Clamorous Reed-Warbler (*Acrocephalus stentoreus*) feeds its hungry young; Metallic Starlings (*Aplonis metallica*) nest in noisy colonies of thousands of individuals. Nests can overwhelm trees; The male Golden-headed Cisticola (*Cisticola exilis*) is very vocal.

# Introduced Birds

Twenty-two species of birds have been introduced into Australia from other countries and become naturalised here. Many of these are well known to Australians, having made themselves at home around cities, suburbs and agricultural areas. Several game-fowl have been introduced as poultry — the Red Junglefowl (*Gallus gallus*), Common Pheasant (*Phasianus colchicus*), Indian Peafowl (*Pavo cristatus*), California Quail (*Callipepla californica*), Chukar Partridge (*Alectoris chukar*), Helmeted Guineafowl (*Numida meleagris*), Mallard (*Anas platyrhynchos*) and Wild Turkey (*Meleagris gallopavo*). The list also includes the familiar House Sparrow (*Passer domesticus*), Eurasian Tree Sparrow (*Passer montanus*); several finches — the European Goldfinch (*Carduelis carduelis*), European Greenfinch (*Carduelis chloris*) and Nutmeg Mannikin (*Lonchura punctulata*); various pigeons and doves — the Feral Pigeon or Rock Dove (*Columba livia*), Spotted Turtle-Dove (*Streptopelia chinensis*), Laughing Turtle-Dove (*Streptopelia senegalensis*); and a number of songbirds — the Common Skylark (*Alauda arvensis*), Red-whiskered Bulbul (*Pycnonotus jocosus*), Common Blackbird (*Turdus merula*), Song Thrush (*Turdus philomelos*), Common Starling (*Sturnis vulgaris*) and Common Myna (*Acridotheres tristis*).

A few of these introductions were accidental (escaping from aviaries), but most were deliberate. Many of these birds are slowly spreading throughout the country, colonising new habitats and creating difficulties for Australia's native birds. For example, the Nutmeg Mannikin (*Lonchura punctulata*) breeds rapidly and out-competes other finch species, particularly the Zebra Finch (*Taeniopygia guttata*) and Double-barred Finch (*Taeniopygia bichenovii*), quickly excluding them from their own habitats. Aviary escapees may have infected the endangered Gouldian Finch (*Erythrura gouldiae*) with the mite that has decimated its populations. Introduced turtle-doves take over the habitats of the native Bar-shouldered Dove (*Geopelia humeralis*) and Peaceful Dove (*Geopelia striata*). The Common Starling (*Sturnus vulgaris*) has increased to pest proportions, creating fire hazards and mite infestations by nesting in roof spaces, as well as overtaking native bird nests. Even the seemingly innocuous House Sparrow (*Passer domesticus*) takes over the nests of the native Fairy Martin (*Hirundo ariel*).

**Opposite:** An Asian species, the Common Myna (*Acridotheres tristis*) was introduced into south-eastern Australia in the 1860s. It also lives in the north-east. **Clockwise from top left:** Female Blackbird (*Turdus merula*) — blackbirds can invade native bushland and compete with native birds; Feral Pigeons (*Columba livia*) originated from Rock Doves but now vary widely due to breeding of different varieties; House Sparrows (*Passer domesticus*) are widespread across Australia but have not yet colonised Western Australia; The Laughing Turtle-Dove (*Streptopelia senegalensis*).

# Birthdwatching

Many Australians have discovered the simple joy of birdwatching. For beginners and dedicated birdwatchers alike, Australia's 750 species offer plenty of scope. Birdwatching is an inexpensive pastime; the required equipment being comfortable earthy-coloured clothes and quiet walking shoes, a hat, sunscreen and sunglasses, a pair of binoculars and/or camera, a notebook and a field guide. If spotting at night for nocturnal birds, a torch or spotlight with red cellophane over the lens is appropriate.

## WHERE AND WHEN TO WATCH

As birds live in all of Australia's habitats including cities and suburbs, suitable places are not hard to find. For best viewing, select a natural site where birds are likely to find food, water, mates and safe nesting sites. This may be in or overlooking a forest, woodland, scrub, swamp, mudflat, dam, farmland, seaside or even a desert. Parks and gardens often have well-used birdbaths or fountains. National parks often have bird hides overlooking wetlands or walking tracks through bird-rich habitats. Remember, during the day birds concentrate their time around water, flowering or fruiting trees or leaf litter.

Diurnal birds are most active in the early morning and from late afternoon until dusk, so these are the best times to hear their calls and watch them. Of course dusk is the start of the night shift, and the next few hours can be productive in terms of watching and enjoying Australia's nocturnal birds. Fewer birds are seen in the middle of the day or in rainy or windy weather.

## TIPS FOR FINDING, OBSERVING AND IDENTIFYING BIRDS

Go alone, with interested friends or family members or join experienced birdwatchers via a local birdwatching club. Find a suitable comfortable place. Stay still and watch quietly. Birds are curious and often come close to investigate people once they are settled. Listen for different birdcalls and the sounds of rustling in branches or on the ground. Follow these auditory clues, using naked vision to locate the bird before smoothly zooming in on it with binoculars. Remember that birds live in or use all the different levels of vegetation including the canopy, middle storeys, undergrowth and leaf litter. At night be sure not to shine light directly into birds' eyes.

Once the bird is within view, take time to look carefully at it, gaining a mental picture of it. The basic task of obtaining a "general impression of shape and size" allows the narrowing down of possibilities for identification. Look for any outstanding or unusual features. Particularly note the size and shape of the bill. Take note of its plumage — the colour and patterns over its various body parts — and behaviours such as twitching or displaying and the way in which it perches, walks or flies. Then consult the field guide and narrow down the options. Use the guide's notes about habitat and distribution maps to identify the species.

Sketching or noting the bird's characteristics in a notebook or field diary helps birdwatchers, both beginners and more experienced, to remember new bird species. It also provides details for later reference, perhaps to check the accuracy of the field identification. Birdwatching groups often conduct surveys and appreciate lists of birds seen by amateurs. Be sure to record the date, time of day, place, weather conditions, birds seen and their behaviours.

## BIRD SAFETY

Be sure not to disturb nests, eggs, chicks or their parents, either by excessive noise, sudden movements or direct interference. Parents sometimes abandon disturbed nests. Be aware that it is illegal to collect eggs or keep protected birds without a permit. Share findings only with like-minded people who will help to protect birds.

**Opposite:** Birdwatching at Mareeba Wetlands offers a chance to see Black-necked Storks and Brolgas. **Above, top to bottom:** Getting close to birds is made easier with portable bird hides; The hide at Boondall Wetlands near Brisbane gives a chance to see large numbers of migratory birds feeding from September to March; Binoculars bring birds a lot closer.

# On the Brink

Humans have always had a mixed relationship with birds, both revered and, on the other hand, hunted for food and feathers. With the colonisation of new lands, pets and domestic animals have impacted on native birds, particularly those that had evolved without ground predators. Perceived as pests, native birds are often killed in agricultural areas. Pollution, food chain contamination, the cage-bird trade, the exploitation of certain species for fishing or hunting purposes, and continued habitat clearing may push already pressured birds to the brink of extinction. Of the world's nearly 10,000 bird species, more than 2000 are threatened or endangered. Refer to www.iucnredlist.org for more information.

In Australia, about 10 native species and 13–14 subspecies have become extinct since European settlement. Over 70 are currently considered Endangered or Critically Endangered, over 80 are Vulnerable and a similar number are Near Threatened. Refer to www.birdsaustralia.com.au for further information.

## CONSERVATION

Conservation is critical to the continued enjoyment of birds. Habitat and species protection are the most fundamental conservation measures. National parks and other substantial natural reserves, including habitat on private land, provide feeding and breeding sites for numerous bird (and other wildlife) species. All native birds are protected in Australia, wildlife trading without permits is illegal, and the use of pesticides and contaminants is regulated. Research into bird behaviour and ecology provides vital information for conservation managers. Captive breeding programs may help save endangered species.

## HOW YOU CAN HELP

Awareness and concern are the keys to conservation. Learn about Australia's wonderful birds. Read books and websites. Join a birdwatching group. Go birdwatching. Share your knowledge and experiences with others. Participate in clean up activities at local revegetation projects, or bird surveys. Report inappropriate treatment of birds. Join a conservation group or donate time or resources.

**Top:** A feral cat devours a bird.
**Right:** Loss of habitat is the biggest threat to all wildlife.

# Birds in Your Backyard

Watching birds in the backyard can be a wonderful up-close-and-personal experience of nature. However, careful thought is required to create a garden that will attract native birds in need of human assistance, rather than aggressive birds that don't need help. The first step is to assess the current backyard situation. Which birds are visiting at which times? Which plants are they using? What are the locally native bird species? Which plants do they require? Consult with local bird groups or native plant nurseries. Once the more desirable local birds and their feeding requirements have been identified, draft a plan. Then in stages remove weeds and replant areas with locally native plants.

It is important to create a structurally complex garden — one that has trees, shrub layers, ground cover, leaf litter, logs and grass. Diversity is also important. A range of plants with smaller flowers that bloom throughout the year will attract smaller birds. Providing larger flowers favours larger more aggressive honeyeaters that tend to chase away smaller birds. Wrens and other insectivorous birds will be attracted to feed amongst the leaf litter and other birds will use it for nesting materials. Include a water feature or birdbath in a safe location and keep it clean. Nesting boxes can be placed in trees out of the wind. Monitor their use to ensure the desired species are using them and not being preyed upon. A bird hide can be constructed to ensure unobstructed viewing in this newly created habitat. Be sure to keep cats and dogs under control. There is little point in attracting birds only to have them scared away by pets. Lastly, remember that it is far better for birds to find their own food than to depend on human intervention. Supplementary feeding has been found to favour aggressive bird species that prey on smaller birds, undoing all the good work. Check out the Birds Australia website (www.birdsaustralia.com.au) for more information.

**Above, left to right:** Insectivorous birds such as this Scarlet Robin catch their prey on or near the ground. Having leaf litter in your garden can help species like these; Providing water can assist but it may be used only by aggressive, dominant birds.

# Glossary

**ALTITUDINAL MIGRATION**
Movement of populations of birds between two different altitudes, usually for breeding purposes.

**ARBOREAL** Tree-dwelling.

**BREEDING PLUMAGE**
Distinctive plumage worn during breeding season.

**BROODING** The process of rearing chicks, keeping them warm and feeding them until they leave the nest.

**CAP** Plumage on a bird's crown.

**COLOUR MORPH**
Distinctively plumed form of a species.

**COUNTER-SHADED** Dark above, light below.

**CROP** A muscular "pouch" that is part of some birds' digestive systems used to temporarily store food.

**CROP MILK** The whitish liquid produced from ingested seeds by some pigeons. Nestlings put their heads inside their parents' crops to drink it.

**CRYPTIC** Of camouflaged patterning or behaviour.

**DISPERSIVE** A species that disperses after rain or with other favourable conditions.

**DIURNAL** Active during the day.

**ECLIPSE** Non-breeding plumage of a male bird.

**ENDEMIC** Native to a certain place and living nowhere else.

**FLANKS** The sides of a bird's belly, nearest to its wings.

**FLEDGLING** A young bird with feathers but as yet unable to fly properly.

**GAPE** The width of a bird's open bill or other animal's open mouth.

**INCUBATION** The process of maintaining a near-constant egg temperature.

**LERPS** Small leaf sucking insects, also known as scale.

**LORES** The plumage or bare skin between the eye and the beak.

**MANNA** Energy rich sugary sap produced by trees after injury by insects.

**MANTLE** The plumage across a bird's shoulders between the wings.

**MOULT** The process of losing older feathers, replacing them with new ones.

**NESTLING** A young bird living in the nest.

**NOCTURNAL** Active during the night.

**NOMADIC** Moving irregularly, usually in response to rainfall and erratic food supplies.

**NON-PASSERINE** Any bird not belonging to the order Passeriformes.

**PARASITE** An animal or plant that lives on another and feeds upon it.

**PASSERINE** A member of the order Passeriformes. A bird with the ability to perch and possibly a songbird.

**PIED** Black and white.

**PLUMAGE** A bird's total covering of feathers, and its general visual impression.

**POWDER DOWN** Waxy substance that grows on the breast, rump or flanks of some bird species. When preening these birds distribute it over their feathers like powder.

**PREDATOR** An animal that hunts and eats other animals.

**PREEN** The act of cleaning and realigning feathers.

**PRIMARY FLIGHT FEATHERS**
The flight feathers on the outer part of a bird's wing, furthest from its body.

**RESIDENT** Non-migratory. Remaining in one place all year.

**ROOST** The place a bird sleeps or congregates with others of its species.

**RUMP** The backside of a bird's body at the base of the tail.

**SCAVENGER** An animal that feeds on the carcasses of dead animals.

**SCRAPE** A bare shallow depression in the ground.

**SECONDARY FLIGHT FEATHERS** The flight feathers on the inner part of a bird's wing, closest to a bird's body.

**SEDENTARY** Remaining in the same area for the entire year or lifetime, except that after breeding young may disperse.

**SPECULUM** Iridescent green-purple patch on a duck's or parrot's wing.

**SYRINX** Vocal organ of a bird; more highly developed in songbirds.

**TALON** Strong claws of birds-of-prey.

**WATTLE** Fleshy lobe hanging from the neck, often becomes brightly coloured during breeding season.

**WINGSPAN** The maximum wingtip-to-wingtip distance of naturally spread wings.

# Index

# Index continued

# Links & Further Reading

## Books

Simpson, K. & Day, N. *Field Guide to the Birds of Australia*, Penguin Group (Australia), Camberwell, Victoria, 2004

Morcombe, M. *Field Guide to Australian Birds. Complete Compact Edition*, Steve Parish Publishing, Brisbane, 2004

Gosler, A (gen. ed.) *Philip's Birds of the World*, Philip's Limited, London, 2006

Burger, J. *Birds: A Visual Guide*, Firefly Books, New York, USA, 2006

Attenborough, D. *The Life of Birds*, BBC Books, London, 1998

Beruldsen, G. *Australian Birds: Their Nests and Eggs*, G. Beruldsen, Brisbane, Qld, 2003

Rohr, I. *Birds of Australia*, New Holland, Chatswood, NSW, 2008

Currey, K. *Australian Birds Fact File*, Steve Parish Publishing, Brisbane, 2007

Cox, K. *Amazing Facts About Australian Birds*, Steve Parish Publishing, Brisbane, 2008

Geering, A., Agnew, L. & Harding, S. *Shorebirds of Australia*, CSIRO Publishing, Melbourne, 2007

## Websites

Birds Australia
www.birdsaustralia.com.au

For information about backyard bird habitats
www.birdsinbackyards.net/

Guidelines for the development of bird habitats
www.birdsinbackyards.net/spaces/guidelines.cfm

Birds in Backyards Survey:
www.birdsinbackyards.net/surveys/

Nesting box information
http://www.birdsinbackyards.net/spaces/bird-needs-resources.cfm#nestboxes

Bird Observers Club of Australia
www.birdobservers.org.au

IUCN Red List of Threatened Species
www.iucnredlist.org

## Acknowledgments

We would like to acknowledge Peter Slater for checking the facts reflected in this book.

Published by Steve Parish Publishing Pty Ltd
PO Box 1058, Archerfield, Qld 4108 Australia
**www.steveparish.com.au**

ISBN 978174193425 0

First published 2009

Principal photography: Steve Parish

Additional photography: Graeme Chapman: pp. 11 (centre right), 25 (top), 74 (top), 75, 95 (bottom), 100 (bottom) & 103 (centre); Greg Harm: pp. 18 (3rd from bottom), 40 (top), 51 (bottom right), 71 (bottom left & right) & 74 (bottom); Jiri Lochman/Lochman Transparencies: p. 106 (top); M & I Morcombe: pp. 5, 13, 31 (top), 43 (centre & bottom), 45 (top), 66 (top), 73 (bottom), 82-83, 93 (bottom right), 97 (centre), 99 (top), 101 (bottom left) & 103 (bottom); Ian Morris: pp. 11 (bottom right), 63 (centre), 64 (bottom), 77 (top), 87 (bottom left) & 94 (top & bottom left); Peter Slater: pp. 43 (top), 60 (bottom), 61 (top), 62 (bottom), 73 (top & centre), 77 (centre left) & 78 (top); Len H. Smith: p. 70 (bottom); Ron & Valerie Taylor: pp. 32 (bottom right) & 34; Clare Thomson: p. 105 (centre); Martin Willis: pp. 71 (top) & 81

Front cover image: New Holland Honeyeater

Title Page: Rainbow Lorikeets. Inset, top to bottom: Southern Boobook; Scarlet Robin

Text: Lynne Adcock
Design: Leanne Nobilio, SPP
Editorial: Kerry McDuling; Jason Negus, Cathy Vallance, Helen Anderson, SPP
Image Library: Clare Thomson, SPP
Production: Tina Brewster, SPP

Prepress by Colour Chiefs Digital Imaging, Brisbane, Australia
Printed in Singapore by Imago

**Produced in Australia at the Steve Parish Publishing Studios**